paper cutting

paper cutting

20 projects for friends to make

super+super

First published 2015 by
Guild of Master Craftsman Publications Ltd
Castle Place, 166 High Street, Lewes,
East Sussex BN7 1XU

Text © Claire Culley and Amy Phipps, 2015
Copyright in the Work © GMC Publications Ltd, 2015

ISBN 978 1 86108 731 7

Publisher: Jonathan Bailey
Production Manager: Jim Bulley
Senior Project Editor: Dominique Page
Editor: Sarah Doughty
Managing Art Editor: Gilda Pacitti
Designer: Simon Goggin
Illustrator: Anna-Kaisa Jormanainen
Photographers: Claire Culley, Harry Watts
and Rebecca Mothersole

Set in Akzidenz-Grotesk, Ani Lazy Day and Calibri
Colour origination by GMC Reprographics
Printed and bound in China

contents

Introduction to paper cutting

Paper is everywhere we look – newspapers, books, magazines, money, to name just a few, are all made from paper. We use it every day for reading, writing lists and sending thank-you notes.

When paper was first invented, making it was a long and extremely delicate process. Papermaking involved macerating the fibre out of plants to make individual strands that could be stuck together with water. As time went on, it was found you could also make paper out of wood and the process became less expensive and time consuming. As the years passed, large-scale production techniques were developed – and large amounts of paper could be produced in a more cost-effective way. By then paper had become an essential item for everyday life.

As well as a practical use, for centuries different cultures have also created the most wonderful art from paper. Origami is probably the most renowned form of paper art, but paper cutting has also been in existence for centuries, evolving in different cultures. It's very exciting today that this art shows no sign of fading away and that modern artists have taken it up to create amazingly delicate pieces of art. Some of these are so fine you would hardly believe they were made from paper!

Paper cutting is an activity that is popular for both children and adults, and you can work together. Most adults have to admit cutting and sticking anything is very creative and always fun! With just a few skills to learn and a wide choice of papers and colours available, artists can create exciting work right from the start.

Paper cutting requires a lot of patience and a steady hand. But once you've got a few tips from us – and a cuppa on the go – there will be no stopping you.

Amy & Claire, Super+Super

Get your scissors out!

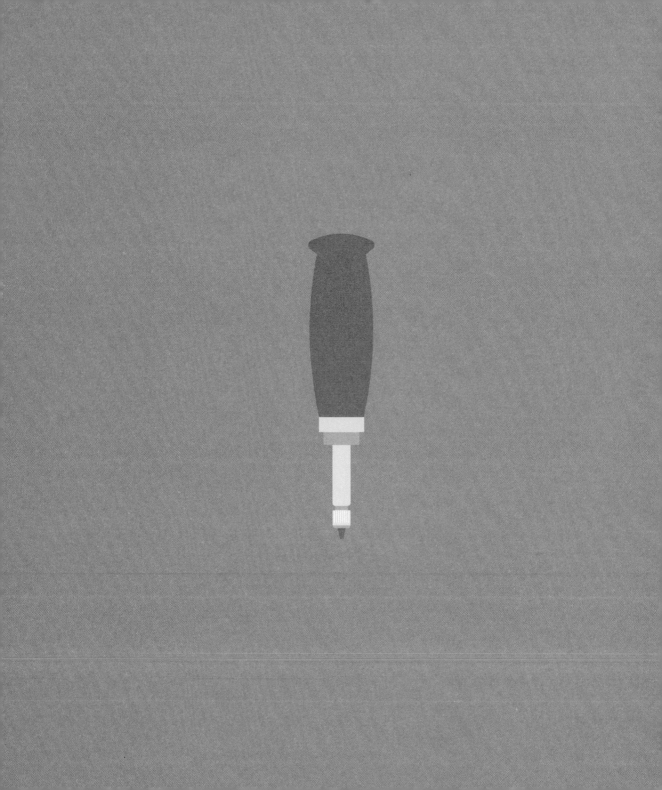

·····*(!)*·····

ready, steady, make

Using this book

This book is a collection of 20 paper-cutting projects of varying levels of difficulty. We would encourage you to personalize each project by choosing your own colours and types of card and so customizing your designs.

Our aim is to help build up your skills and your confidence in paper cutting. We would also encourage you to add in anything extra to your design if you wish to. By the end of this book you will be a pro paper cutter who doesn't flinch when they see a super-intricate design.

We hope this book helps you to develop your own paper-cutting personality and arms you with enough new ideas to make exciting projects of your own. The possibilities for paper cutting are endless. You can make your own greeting cards, decorations, wall art and so much more.

The book is divided into four sections – lazy crafter, weekend winner, perpetual creative and committed crafter. The sections are based on timescales so you can make sure you have enough time to finish one project before you start.

Lazy crafter
These give you a few simple makes for the minimum time and effort. These projects are great for getting you into the swing of something new or for a quick creative fix when you have a few precious moments to spare.

Weeknight winners
This chapter has a selection of projects that are short enough to be completed in a single evening and can be made from items that are readily available around your own home. They are ideal for an evening on your own or to do with a group of friends at a crafty get-together.

Perpetual creative
These medium-length projects will keep you inspired over a quiet weekend (or two) when you need a creative intermission to an often hectic working week.

Committed crafter
These longer-length, more complex projects can be enjoyed at your leisure over an extended period of time, perhaps over a holiday. They are perfect for improving your confidence and skills base.

Before you start paper cutting, you need to make sure you have a flat surface to work from. Ideally you should be at a desk or at your kitchen table. It needs to be somewhere with a smooth surface that's comfortable for you to sit at. Some of the projects can be quite time consuming, so it's important to have a good chair to support your back. Proximity to your kettle is also key as you'll need lots of tea breaks!

Paper cutting requires lots of patience so don't be too disheartened if it takes you a little time to get to grips with it. It may be a good idea to start with the lazy crafter projects to build up your confidence. If you do make a mistake, do not fear. We'll show you exactly how to hide it so no one would ever know.

Once you've got a few of the projects under your belt, why not invite your pals over and teach them your newfound skills? If you are planning a party or upcoming wedding, it's the perfect opportunity to get everyone together to make some party accessories. This book is full of them!

1 *2* *3* *4* *5* *6* *7* *8* *9* *10* *11* *12*

What you'll need

The great thing about paper cutting is that it doesn't require lots of tools or materials. Sure, you may have to buy a few things but most of what you'll need you'll probably already have in your pencil case. As always, a lot of these materials can be picked up at a reasonable cost and if there's a group of you working together you can all club together and buy in bulk, which is always cheaper.

Pick up what you need from art stores, craft shops and local stationers – and anything you can't find will be available online.

basic kit

1 Acrylic paint
Little tubes of acrylic paint are always good to have to hand when working with card or paper. They are quick to dry, easy to apply and always give a great finish.

2 Paintbrushes
You'll only need two types of paintbrush for these projects – a fine one for gluing anything intricate and another brush about 1¼in (2cm) wide for general use.

3 Wooden skewers
Grab some skewers from your local supermarket. They make excellent prop holders and are also handy for punching holes through crêpe paper.

4 String
The choice of string is up to you – you can have plain, coloured or patterned. We've used string for some of the hanging projects (but you could use leftover yarn, too).

5 Eraser
Always have an eraser to hand to correct any little errors you may make.

6 Scissors
A general-purpose pair of scissors is all that you need.

7 Set square
A set square is ideal for making sure you've drawn the correct angles. You can pick one up from any stationers.

8 Embroidery needle
A sharp embroidery needle is ideal for sewing through paper or making small holes.

9 Ruler
A metal ruler is a great asset to any paper cutter, but if you don't have one, a regular ruler will be just fine.

10 Pencil and pen
There's no need for an expensive pencil here; a regular pencil will do just fine. Have a pen to hand too, just in case you need to draw or trace more defined lines.

11 Pom-poms
No crafter's kit would be complete without a pack of pom-poms. Mini pom-poms are great for accessorizing your work and adding a bit of fun to your projects.

12 Embroidery hoop
If you're an avid sewer, your old embroidery hoops make great bases for hanging mobiles. If you don't have a hoop, keep an eye out for them at car boot sales – or you could ask a friend or family member for a spare one.

sticking and fixing

1   Spray-on adhesive

More commonly known as spray glue, this adhesive allows you to spray glue over a large surface for an instant bond. It's clear too, so great for sticking paper to glass or ceramics.

2   Flower-arranging wire

This is a flexible sturdy wire, used in the making of paper flowers. It can also add extra support to your work if you would like it to be freestanding.

3   Flower-arranging tape

This tape is available in different colours and is perfect for making paper flowers. Simply stretch it out to activate it before wrapping around wire to make a stem.

4   PVA

This stands for polyvinyl acetate, which is a rubbery synthetic polymer. It's the most widely recognized glue and is used for sticking any porous material such as paper, card and fabrics. It is white when wet, but dries clear.

5   Latex-based glue

Latex-based glue (which is instantly identified by its fishy smell), is used for many of the projects. It's useful for sticking a variety of materials, such as paper, board, upholstery and carpet. It's also non-toxic, so great for kids to use.

6   Sticky pads

Double-sided sticky pads are used for adding depth to your work. They give a great 3D effect to layered card designs.

7   Masking tape

This is used for securing cutting templates. Buy good-quality tape if you can, so it holds everything where you need it to be.

8   Thread

Standard embroidery thread is all you need here. Pick your favourite colour to use in the hanging projects.

9   Nylon string

Commonly known as fishing wire, this is used as invisible thread for hanging projects. It can be quite fiddly to use, but the results are worth it.

10 Adhesive tape

Sticky tape is a must for paper cutting. It can be used to hold templates in place, secure papers together and for fixing the odd mistake.

Tip! Apply glue in small amounts to help reduce potential spillages and the risk of it showing on your finished project.

cutting

1 Blades
Find a non-surgical blade that is small and straight to use for the projects in this book (blade 10A is ideal).

2 Pliers
Use pliers to safely attach and remove detachable blades from your scalpel handle. This will prevent any little accidents and protect your fingers.

3 Scalpel
For the more complicated projects, it is best to use a scalpel with detachable blades, which you must change frequently. These can be bought from any good arts and crafts shop.

4 Japanese screw punch
This useful punching tool comes with tips to punch different-sized holes through sheets of card with ease.

5 Craft knife
A craft knife with a fixed blade is great for many quick projects. Craft knives are easy to use. You should dispose of them safely once they become blunt.

6 Cutting mat
A cutting mat is a must-have item for paper cutting. Mats come in a variety of sizes and colours, usually with a grid. Choose a mat that suits your needs and workspace.

Tip! Some of the tools you'll need for the projects are very sharp, so use them with caution. If working with children, try to use safer substitutes such as safety scissors.

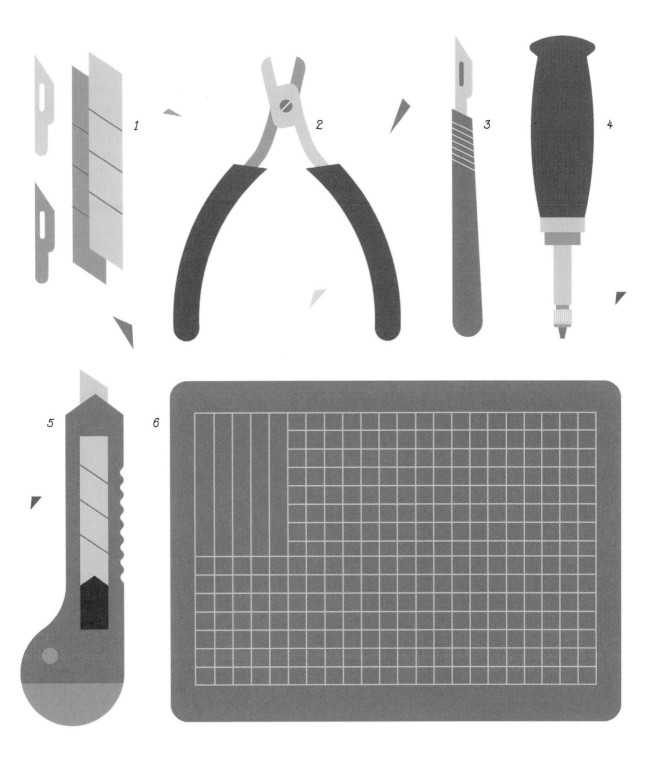

1

2

3

4

5

6

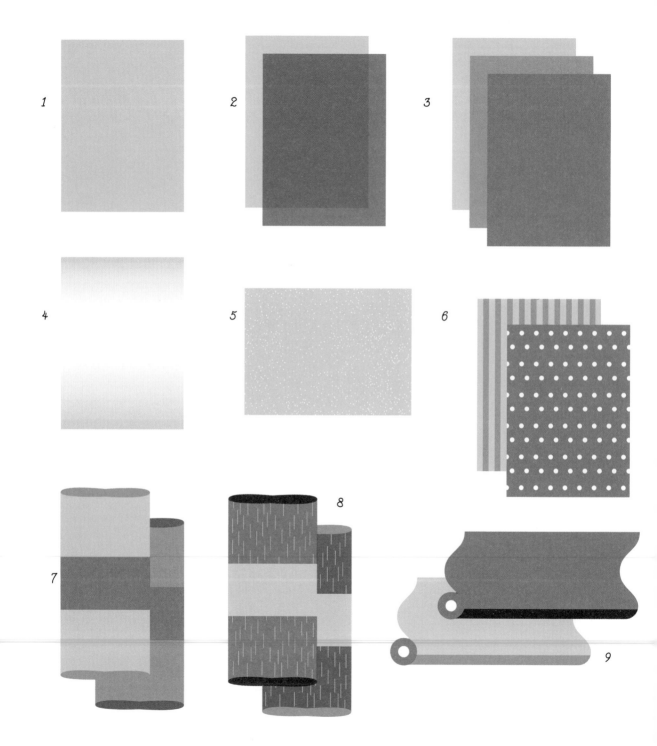

paper and card

Different weights and types of paper and card have been used for the projects – depending on how fine or firm the finished piece needs to be. Most places in the world use ISO paper sizes, measured in grammes per square metre (gsm), ranging in size from A6, the smallest, to A0, the biggest. The US and Canada use a different system of paper sizes and are measured by their basis weight – the weight of a ream (500 sheets) in pounds (lbs). While slightly smaller in size, US Letter size paper is the closest equivalent to A4, the size most often used in this book.

1   Paper

The majority of projects in this book use standard printer/copier paper for doodling designs and making templates – which is A4 (or US Letter size). Most paper today is manufactured from recycled materials and we would encourage you to source recycled paper for all of your projects.

Tip! Be thrifty by keeping hold of any scrap paper and card left over from finished projects – you never know when they'll come in handy for future projects.

2   Tracing paper

Tracing paper has a very low opacity, so light is able to pass through it. This transparency makes it an ideal paper to use for tracing stencils and templates.

3   Card

The projects use a mixture of thin and thick card. Most need a medium-weight card at 160gsm (60lb), which is perfect for crafting. For some of the intricate single-cut projects we've opted for 180gsm (65lb). These projects require a card that is a bit more sturdy, but not too painful for you to cut into for long periods of time. For heavier weight, we've gone for 200gsm (80lb), which is ideal for hanging projects. Do be sure to make use of scraps of leftover card too.

4   Gold foil paper

Gold foil paper is available on rolls and is generally used for decorating objects via heat transfer to give a lovely gold effect. But gold foil has a shiny vibrancy and can be used as a paper. You could use metallic tissue paper as an alternative, if you prefer.

5   Hammered card

This is a card with a slight bumpy effect on one side, adding a bit more texture and interest to a design.

6   Patterned paper

Buy a pack of patterned paper to have in your craft box. It's generally light to medium weight, which makes it great for folding. Patterned paper is useful for origami projects.

7   Tissue paper

Tissue paper is very lightweight and is widely used for delicate craft projects. It's generally made from recycled paper pulp and it's great for scrunching, sticking, wrapping and decorating.

8   Crêpe paper

This is tissue paper that has been given a coating with a glue-like substance and then crêped. It's great for kids' projects and it's also good for making textured pieces. It can be quite hard to cut neatly though, so it's not an ideal medium for making intricate paper cuts.

other material

9   Vinyl

Vinyl is a very versatile plastic polymer. It is synthetic but it is also recyclable, which makes it environmentally friendly. For the projects you will need a blackboard-effect vinyl (which accepts chalk markings) and frosted window vinyl, used for covering glass. Vinyl is available from hardware shops and online.

How to do it

In this section we'll give you a brief overview of the techniques used in the book for paper cutting and transferring stencils, so you can work effectively when you start diving into the projects.

Using a craft knife or scalpel

The easiest and most comfortable way to use a knife is to hold it with your drawing hand and as if it was a pen or pencil. Use your forefinger to control the knife, your thumb to guide it and your middle finger to support it. If you like, you could wrap some tape or a cushioned plaster around the base of the knife to add a bit of cushioning for your fingers.

For easy work, a disposable craft knife with a fixed blade is fine, but it is worth investing in a scalpel with detachable blades for more intricate work. When the blade gets blunt you can remove it, discard it safely and attach a sharp new one. Using a knife can be very dangerous so please take extra care at all times, especially when removing and attaching blades.

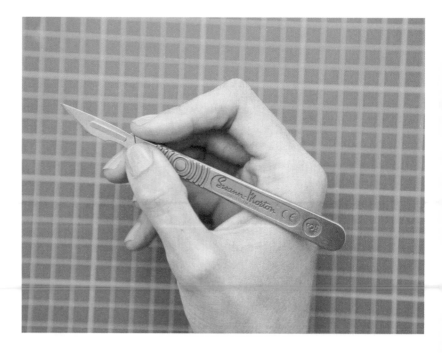

Attaching and removing blades

1 To attach a new blade, first carefully unwrap it from its packaging. Take it out of the packaging using your pliers and hold it along the back edge, with the blade pointing away from you.

2 Pick up the handle in your other hand and bring it close to the blade.

3 You will see that the handle has two built-in grooves on either side. Position the blade in the grooves.

4 Move the handle and blade down towards your cutting mat so the blade and handle are now vertical to the mat.

5 Push the blade down firmly into the mat to pop the blade into position.

6 To remove old blades, grip the blade with your pliers in between the handle and the blade. Slowly lift the blade up and push it away as you do. The blade will then slide off. Be sure to dispose of it carefully.

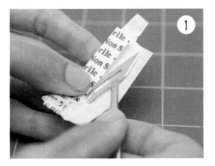

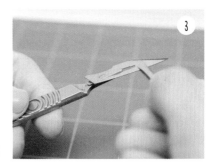
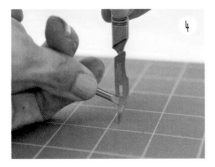

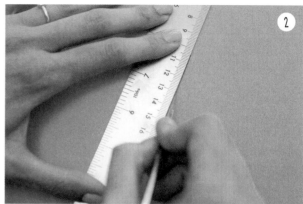

cutting straight lines

The easiest way to cut perfectly straight lines is to use a ruler as a guideline. The more confident you become, the easier you'll find it to do lines freehand. However, if you want a perfectly straight line, then using a ruler is the best way to go.

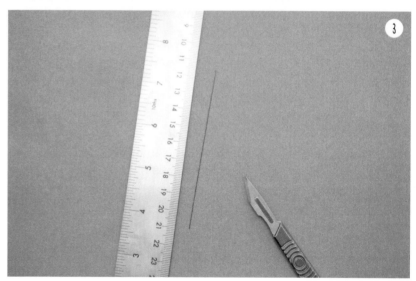

1 Begin by positioning the ruler along the edge of the line you wish to cut. Holding the ruler in place with one hand use the other hand to guide the knife. Bring the blade to the edge of the ruler so it is touching.

2 Pressing firmly with the knife, begin to cut the line, keeping the knife touching the side of the ruler at all times.

3 Try to make the cut in one smooth motion so it's nice and neat. Remove the ruler to reveal your perfectly straight line cut.

cutting corners

When cutting corners, you need to make sure the angles are absolutely correct and the lines are smooth so the corner point looks precise. The best way to do this is to cut the second line slightly longer than needed at the point they cross.

1 Begin to cut the first line for the corner, using your ruler as a guide.

2 Position the paper so you can cut comfortably. When starting the second line, begin cutting just before the first line finishes.

3 Follow the ruler as a guide to complete the cut.

4 This will create a perfectly sharp corner edge.

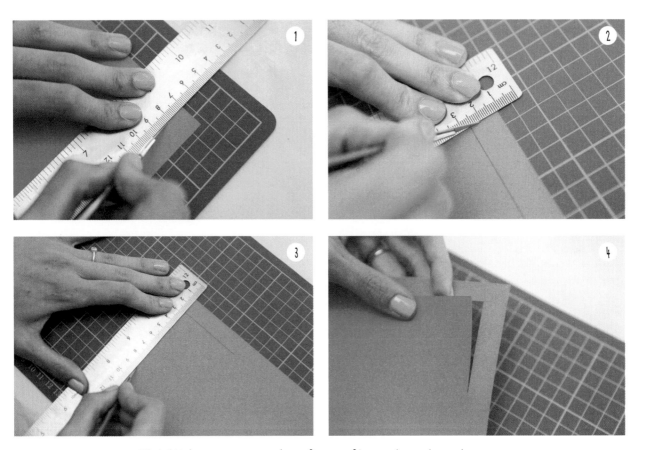

Tip! Make sure your work surface is flat and sturdy and you are concentrating on what you are cutting. Safety first!

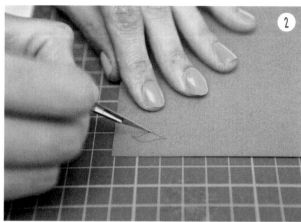

cutting curves

Curves can be tricky to master as you will need to cut them freehand. You should mark the curve you require on the page before starting to cut with your knife.

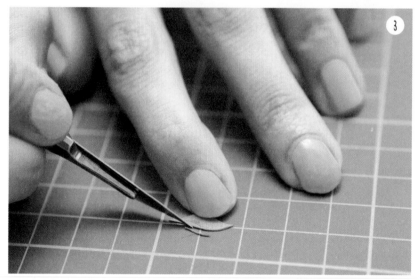

1 With larger curves, move the paper clockwise at intervals rather than twisting your arm too far. This will ensure that you retain optimum control over the knife.

2 With smaller curves, lots of small little cuts are the key. Rather than trying to bend your arm to do a small curve, make little cuts, one after the other.

3 Any edges can always be neatened up afterwards.

Tip! Practise on scrap paper until you feel confident.

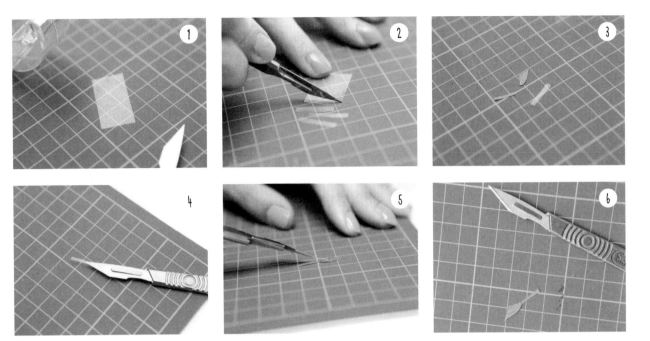

fixing mistakes

Don't worry if you make a mistake and cut somewhere you shouldn't. Sticky tape was made to fix this problem. If you do an extra cut by accident or cut a piece off by mistake, all you need to do is cut a piece of tape small enough to stick it back on.

1 Stick a bit of tape to your cutting mat and pick up your scalpel.

2 Cut the tape into small strips (or whatever size you need).

3 Turn over your pieces of card and locate the area that needs to be put back together.

4 Using the end of your blade lift up the tape onto the end.

5 Use the knife to place the tape onto the cut or to fix the piece back together.

6 Press down firmly with your finger afterwards to secure. Turn the card back over and you'd never know there had been a mishap.

Transferring templates

Most of the projects in this book offer templates so you can copy the design and recreate it yourself. We encourage you to personalize the templates or even draw your own – but if not, you will need to transfer them onto your medium ready for cutting. You can trace the templates using either tracing paper or thin scrap paper. There are three methods to do this:

Paper rubbing

This is an effective way of transferring a drawing onto card. Be aware that the stencil will end up showing the reverse image, so is most useful for symmetrical images.

1   To paper rub your template, you first need to draw over it on a piece of tracing paper (or thin scrap paper) using a pencil.

2   Take your medium and place the tracing paper on the top with the pencil side face down.

3   Use your pencil to etch over the back of the lines.

4   You will have transferred the pencil on the underneath of the tracing paper onto the card below.

Indenting

A way to get around producing a negative image is to indent the design onto your card. This is useful for letters, words and numbers.

1   Simply trace the template as normal using a pencil or pen on tracing paper or scrap paper.

2   Move the tracing paper over your card and using a very sharp pencil or a pen draw over the image again. This time make sure you press quite firmly.

3   This will create an indent in your paper once you've removed the tracing paper. This gives you a guide to work from without any pencil marks.

Tip! A 4H pencil will work best for this, but it's fine if you only have an HB pencil – you might just need to press a little harder.

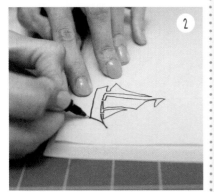

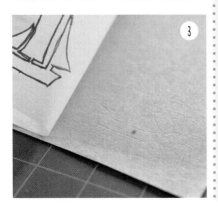

Stencilling

If the design is too detailed for the indenting method to work well, try this stencilling method.

1   Trace the design onto a piece of tracing paper using a pen or pencil.

2   Using some sticky tape, attach the tracing paper to the design in all four corners. Make sure you peel the tape on and off a fabric surface first so it is slightly fluffy and less likely to stick to the card.

3   Use your scalpel to cut through both the tracing paper and the card at the same time. Take extra care to make sure the tracing paper is in the right place at all times.

To use the templates in this book

You will find the templates needed for the projects at the back. Most of the templates are at 100 per cent size. Just follow the directions for transferring the template to your medium in the steps. Most of the templates can be transferred using the rubbing or indenting method.

For the templates that have been reproduced at a smaller size, increase the size on a photocopier as indicated, then follow the directions in the steps.

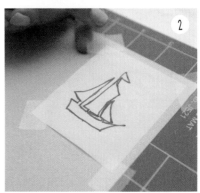

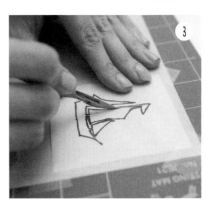

؛\¡/؛/ ! \؛\¡/؛

lazy crafter

¿/!\؛\ ¡ /؛/!\¿

Birthday-cake toppers

Create these simple and stylish decorations to jazz up a birthday cake. Birthday-cake toppers are quick and easy to make, so why not make all the numbers and keep them in a drawer? You'll never be caught short when it comes to an impromptu birthday celebration.

WHAT YOU NEED

- ☐ Scrap paper for stencil
- ☐ 160gsm A4/60lb US Letter size card stock in orange and colours of your choice
- ☐ Pencil
- ☐ Pen
- ☐ Cutting mat
- ☐ Craft knife
- ☐ Sticky tape
- ☐ Wooden skewers

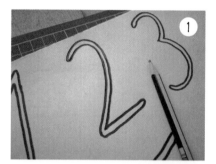

1 Trace the templates you require (see pages 122–123) onto scrap paper in pencil and again in pen if you like. Lay your first stencil over the top of your piece of card and trace over it again. Be sure to push quite hard so it indents through onto the card.

2 Remove the stencil to show your markings and pencil over them to provide a clearer outline of the number/s.

3 Making sure your card is on your cutting mat, use your craft knife to slowly cut around the number. Once you reach the end the number should easily lift out.

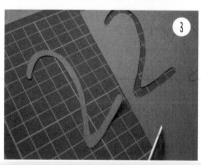

Tip! It's just as simple to make letter toppers, so why not make the words 'Happy Birthday' to add to your cake decorations?

4 Repeat this process for the other number, if using. You can now go round the edges of each of the numbers to improve any areas that are slightly uneven.

5 Cut off a piece of sticky tape around ½in (2cm) long and stick it to your cutting mat. Cut a strip of tape around ⁵⁄₆₄in (2mm) wide. Pick one of your numbers, turn it over and place the end of a skewer onto it. Now lay your strip of tape over the back of the skewer to secure it. Press firmly around the skewer to make sure it is firmly in position.

6 Attach the other number to a second skewer, if using. Now you can decorate your cake.

Party props

WHAT YOU NEED

- [ ] Scrap paper for stencil
- [ ] 160gsm A4/60lb US Letter size card stock in black and mixed colours
- [ ] Pencil
- [ ] Pen
- [ ] Cutting mat
- [ ] Craft knife
- [ ] Washi tape
- [ ] Skewer

Create these fun party props for a special occasion. They are quick and simple to make, so perfect for a photobooth at your wedding, birthday or anniversary. There is a variety of stencils to choose from, or why not make up your own?

1   Choose your templates from the fun range of props (see page 124) with a variety of card colours. Trace the templates you have chosen onto scrap paper in pencil and go over them with a pen if you like. Lay each stencil over the top of your piece of card and trace over it again. Make sure you push quite hard so that it indents the card.

2   Remove the stencil and use your pencil to draw over the indent. This will make it a lot clearer for when you cut out the prop.

3   Place your piece of card onto the cutting mat and pick up your craft knife. You can use scissors here if you want to, but a craft knife gives a precise edge. Start to cut your prop out slowly, taking extra care in any fiddly areas. Remove the prop from the rest of the card.

4   Turn over the prop and cut a piece of tape. Press the tape over the back of the skewer to secure it to the card.

5   Turn back over and your prop is finished. Repeat this process until all your props are made. Try varying it with different coloured cards and the different stencils provided. Happy snapping!

Tip! Place the stencil as close to the edge of the card as you can, so you maximize the number of props you can get out of one piece of card, reduce wastage and help to save the environment, too!

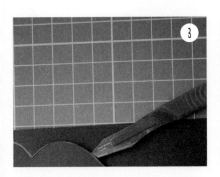

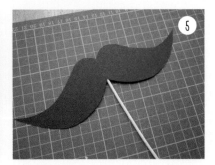

Crown party hats

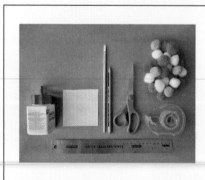

WHAT YOU NEED

- [ ] 180gsm sheet of A1/65lb card in grey
- [ ] Pencil
- [ ] Scrap paper for stencil
- [ ] Scissors
- [ ] A pack of small pom-poms
- [ ] Glue
- [ ] Paintbrush
- [ ] Sticky tape
- [ ] Ruler

Tip! Have fun with your pom-poms and place them wherever you like — they look great at either the top or bottom of the crown.

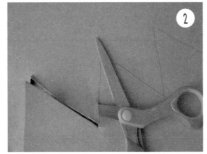

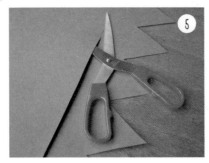

These royal party hats are not just for kids. No way! Add a bit of fun to your own birthday party proceedings with these pom-pom crown party hats. One piece of A1 card is enough to make six hats. Grab your pom-poms and get gluing!

1 First create a simple template from scrap paper. Draw a triangle 2½in (6cm) wide and 2½in (6cm) high. Place your piece of card onto the card, 1½in (4cm) from the long edge. Using a ruler to help you position the triangles, use a pencil to draw around your template going across the width of the card.

2 Using the scissors, start to cut out the line you have just drawn. Take extra care when cutting it out as you are going to re-use the diagonal-shaped line to make another crown. Once cut out, hold it up to your head and wrap it round to work out how long it needs to be. Use the scissors to snip it at the length you need.

3 Grab your pom-poms, glue and a paintbrush and get sticking! You just need a blob of glue on each pom-pom.

4 Start sticking the pom-poms along the base of the crown until the full length is covered. We've alternated our colours, but you can just do a solid

colour if you'd prefer. Leave to dry for a few minutes, then use a piece of sticky tape to secure the two ends together to form a crown shape.

5 Going back to your piece of card you'll see that the top of another crown has already been cut out, making it as easy as pie to do another. Simply pop a ruler onto the point of one of the crown tips and measure 4in (10cm). Do this a few times along the length of the card and join up the dots into a long line. Cut out the line you have just drawn and repeat steps 3–6.

6 *Voila!* Two party hats made in half an hour.

Valentine's cards

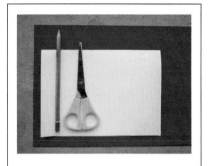

WHAT YOU NEED

- [ ] 180gsm A4/ 65lb US Lettercard in red and gold
- [ ] Pencil
- [ ] Scrap paper for stencil
- [ ] Scissors

1 Start by folding the red card into thirds. This ensures you that get the maximum number of cards out of one sheet.

2 Trace the template (see page 125) onto scrap paper. Lay your stencil over the top of your piece of red card and trace over it again. Be sure to leave space along the fold so it stays together when you cut it out. Alternatively, you can draw the heart shape freehand.

3 Use the scissors to cut out the first heart shape.

4 Your first card is now finished. Now cut out the rest of the hearts along the same row. You can also repeat each step again using the gold card.

5 All that's left to do now is grab a pen and start scribbling your love letters: 'From your secret admirer', or 'to my special friend'.

Send a card to your loved one, but who said Valentine's Day was just for romance? Why not make lots of little cards and send them to your best friends as well? They are so quick to make and perfect for sending little bits of love in the post.

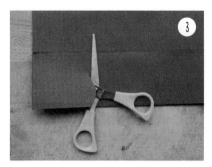

Blackboard stickers

WHAT YOU NEED

☐ Scrap paper for stencils
☐ Pencil
☐ Sheet of adhesive vinyl
  blackboard paper
☐ Scissors
☐ Chalks

These quick and easy blackboard stickers are ideal for decorating your studio space, your kitchen or hallway. Stick them up anywhere you'd like to write a reminder or a quick hello. We've gone for a thought bubble, but once you've got the hang of it you can make all kinds of shapes and silhouettes.

1   Trace the template onto scrap paper (see page 126). Lay your stencil over the top of your vinyl and trace over it again. Alternatively, if you feel comfortable with your drawing skills you can draw the shape freehand.

2   Repeat this process to draw the two small circle shapes onto the back of the blackboard paper. Try to keep them as close as possible to the edge of the bubble shape. This way you'll be able to get more than one sticker out of the sheet.

3   Use the scissors to start cutting out the big bubble shape. Be sure to take extra care in the fiddly areas.

4   Once you've cut out the big bubble you can now cut out the small circle shapes. Do this one by one, and put everything to one side.

5   Now all your shapes are cut out you can lay them on your work surface and plan how you want to stick them on the wall. Once you are ready, all you need to do is slowly peel off the backing to reveal your sticker.

6   Simply place the sticker on the wall and press using medium pressure to secure. Repeat with the two circles, too. These are ready for you to draw on with chalks to your heart's content!

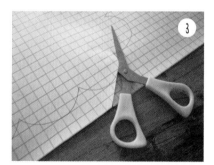

RUSSIAN DOLL, PAGE 70

BIRD WALL-HANGING, PAGE 88

(weeknight winners)

Party garland

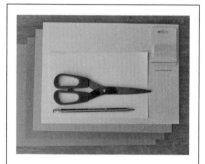

This bold geometric garland is the perfect decoration for any party, celebration or DIY wedding. It makes a 23ft (7m) garland, which is long enough to decorate a ceiling or doorway. You could even use it as a photobooth backdrop along with our fun party props.

WHAT YOU NEED

- ☐ Scrap paper or card for stencil
- ☐ Pencil
- ☐ 160gsm A4/60lb US Letter size card stock in yellow, blue, orange and pink
- ☐ Scissors
- ☐ 23ft (7m) of nylon string
- ☐ Sharp embroidery needle

1 Create a simple template from scrap paper or card. Draw a triangle 2½in (6cm) wide and 2½in (6cm) high.

2 Use the scissors to cut it out.

3 Take your first sheet of card and lay it horizontally on your table. Pop the template onto the bottom left-hand corner and draw round it with a pencil. Tessellate the triangle and repeat; the triangle should be upside down this time.

4 Continue this along the width of the paper and then do the same on the row above.

5 Repeat until the sheet is covered. You should end up with 24 triangle shapes drawn on the card.

6 Use your scissors to cut out each triangle, one by one. Once finished you will have 24 cut-out triangles.

7 Repeat steps 3–6 with the other three colours of card. Collect all the triangles together, ready to sew them together.

8 Take the nylon string and thread it onto your needle. Take one triangle and, using the needle, push up through the bottom of the card in the centre.

9 Do a simple running stitch, using two stitches on each triangle piece. Push the needle back down through the card about ⅜in (1cm) along from where you originally came up. Pull it through and come back up another ⅜in (1cm) along the card. Push the needle back through the card another ⅜in (1cm) along, to create two stitches in the card.

10 Now take a different coloured triangle. Join the cards together with the nylon string, again sewing along the triangle. Repeat and as you work, slide the triangles further down the nylon string. Leave about ⅜in (1cm) space in between each triangle.

11 Try rotating the triangles in different directions to add variety to the garland as you go along.

12 Continue to sew all the triangles onto the nylon string. It may help to do a section at a time, before pushing it all along and carrying on with the next section. Take care not to tangle the nylon string. Finally, tie knots at each end, leaving about 20in (50cm) at each end for hanging.

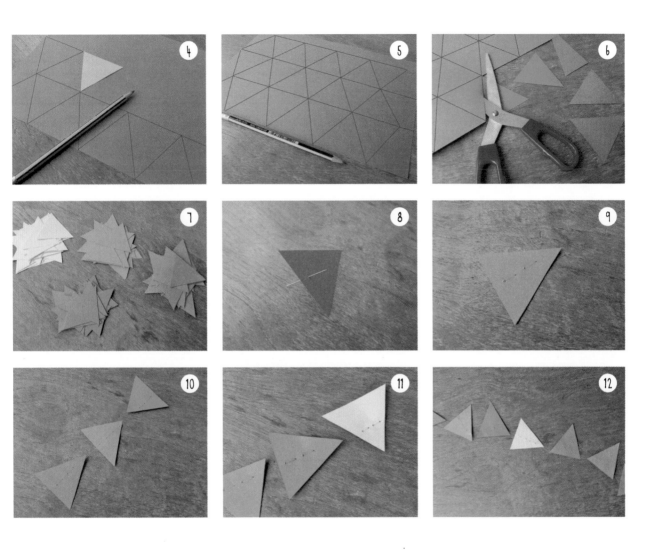

Tip! There are no rules, so you don't have to stick with the triangles we've used — mix it up with as many different shapes as you like.

Cloud baby mobile

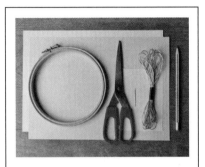

Help your little one drift off to sleep with this calming baby mobile. Reuse an old embroidery hoop to create this simple yet stylish design. Hang the mobile over your baby's cot or as a decorative accessory in your baby's room – either way he or she will be on cloud nine!

WHAT YOU NEED

- [ ] Scrap paper for stencil
- [ ] Pencil
- [ ] Scissors
- [ ] 180gsm A4/65lb US Letter size card stock in pale blue and white
- [ ] Sharp embroidery needle
- [ ] Metallic gold thread
- [ ] 6in (16cm) embroidery hoop

1 Trace the template (see page 127) onto scrap paper. Lay your stencil over the top of your piece of card and trace over it again to indent the shape. Make the outline clear with a pencil.

2 Use the scissors to cut out the shape you've just drawn.

3 Starting with the pale blue card, trace around the template you've made. Make sure it is as close to the edges of the card as possible.

4 Draw six cloud shapes onto the blue card and four shapes onto the white card using your template.

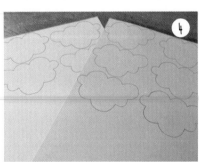

5   Using the scissors, begin to cut out the cloud shapes.

6   Once all the shapes have been cut out, arrange them on your work surface ready to start assembling.

7   Start by taking two of the white clouds and make a vertical cut to the middle of each cloud.

8   Slot the two clouds together.

9   Repeat this process until you have five 3D clouds.

10 Cut a length of thread around 18in (45cm) long. Place the thread on the table and open up the end to loosen the thin threads. Pull out five separate threads and pop the rest to one side for later.

Tip! This baby mobile would make a wonderful gift for a loved one's new arrival.

11 Take one of the thin threads you have separated and tie a double knot in one end.

12 Thread the other end onto your needle and push the needle through the top of one of the clouds. Pull the thread all the way through so it can now hang.

13 Repeat this using the threads for the rest of the clouds.

14 Open out your embroidery hoop and remove the outer hoop and put it to one side. Begin knotting the first hanging cloud onto the rim. Now work your way around the hoop knotting each cloud at an even interval. Stagger the lengths of the clouds to make sure you are tying some longer than the others. The lengths of hanging string on this mobile are 18in (45cm), 12in (30cm), 11in (28cm) and 2 x 8in (20cm).

15 Once all your clouds are attached you now need to attach more string to this inner rim so it can hang. Go back to your gold thread and take four more strands. Cut them all at a suitable hanging length, around 18in (45cm). Knot them onto the inner rim at even intervals.

16 Push the knots around to the outside of the inner hoop and place the outer hoop over the top of the inner hoop. This will conceal all the knots you've made. Tighten the hoop to secure. Now tie a knot in the end of the four hanging threads and trim off any excess thread at the end and your mobile is ready to hang.

Watermelon stationery set

WHAT YOU NEED

- [ ] 200gsm A4/80lb US Letter size card stock in red
- [ ] Scalpel
- [ ] Pencil
- [ ] Scrap paper for stencils
- [ ] Cutting mat
- [ ] 180gsm A4/65lb US Letter size card stock in green, white and black
- [ ] Latex-based glue
- [ ] Small paintbrush

Send a bit of joy in the post with these easy-to-make fruity rocking cards. The bright, fun design will bring a smile to anyone's face. Perfect for thank-you cards, birthday-party invites or just a happy note to your best pal.

1   Take the red piece of card and fold in half lengthways. With great care, use the side of the scalpel (or a ruler) to push down along the fold to score.

2   Trace the templates (see page 128) onto scrap paper. Lay stencil A over the top of your piece of red card and trace over it again, making sure that the flat side of it is parallel to the folded side. You can fit two designs onto this one piece of card.

3   Keeping the card on the cutting mat, slowly but carefully cut out the first semicircle you have drawn with a scalpel. Push down quite firmly to ensure that the blade cuts through both parts of the card.

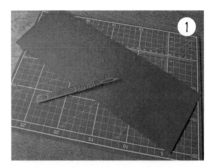

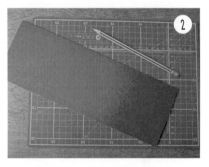

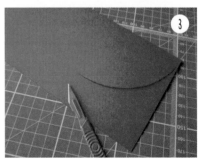

4 Repeat the same process as step 3 with the second semicircle you have drawn.

5 Take the green piece of card next and draw on stencil B. Once again, you can fit two stencils onto the card.

6 Using a scalpel, cut out one of the semicircles. Keep the cutting action fluid to create a clean line. Repeat the same process with the second semicircle and pop them to one side for later.

7 Now take the white piece of card and draw on stencil C. Once again, you can get two on one side of the card.

8 Use the scalpel to cut them both out and pop them with the rest for sticking later.

9 Now cut out the watermelon seeds (stencil D). Stencil 10 seeds onto a piece of black card, close to the edge. Use the scalpel to cut out the seeds one by one. Keep them safe as they have a tendency to get lost or fly off the table when you're not looking!

10 Gather one of the red, green and white cutouts, five of the seeds, the glue and your paintbrush. Cover the table with a protective surface (we've just used our cutting mat but you could use a piece of newspaper or scrap paper).

11 First of all, you need to stick the white cutout onto the red card. Dip your paintbrush lightly into the glue and dab it all across the back of the white cutout. Open out the red card and place the white cutout glue-side down onto the edge of the red card. Press it down firmly to secure.

12 Repeat the process with the green cutout. This time you are sticking the green layer onto the edge of the white.

13 Next grab a seed, turn it over and using your paintbrush blob a small bit of glue onto the back.

14 Stick the first seed in the centre of the red card. Make sure you are sticking it down so the shape resembles a teardrop. Do the same with the other seeds.

15 Repeat the steps with the other pieces you have cut out to make the second card. Don't worry if there are a few bits of glue seeping out. It dries pretty quickly and you can then pick off any visible bits.

Tip! The instructions make two cards at the same time. To make more, simply increase the quantity of card you use. Keep all the leftover card and cutout bits to make more cards in the future.

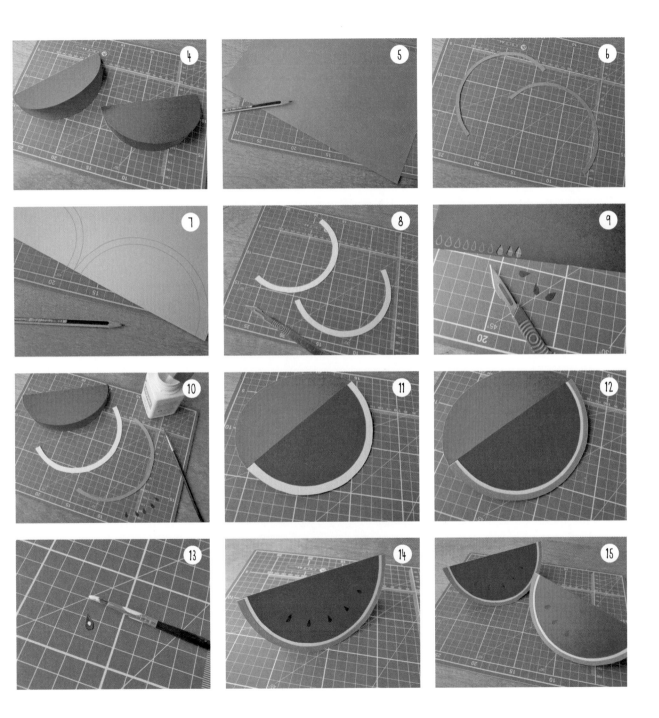

Crêpe-paper flowers

WHAT YOU NEED

- [ ] Crêpe paper in mixed colours of your choice
- [ ] Scissors
- [ ] 7in (18cm) green flower-arranging wire
- [ ] Sticky tape
- [ ] Green flower-arranging tape
- [ ] Skewer

Tip! Why not try creating different sizes of flower to add variety to your bouquet?

These lovely anemone crêpe-paper flowers brighten up any table-top or mantelpiece. You could even make them into a bouquet. They last all year and what's more, they are made without using glue so there is no glue fuss and no drying time.

1 Take your first colour of crêpe paper ready to make the pollen centre of the flower. Use scissors to cut a rectangular shape 7in (18cm) long by 2½in (6cm) wide.

2 Now make strands into the crêpe paper with a spacing of about ¼in (5mm) along one side. Be sure to leave ¾in (2cm) of uncut space along the other side. Keep working along the width of the crêpe paper. This is going to be rolled up to make the inside of your flower.

3 Grab your flower-arranging wire and cut it to about 7in (18cm) long. Place the wire at the edge of the crêpe paper.

4 Begin to roll up the wire and the paper away from you. Keep it as tight as possible; it may help to keep pinching it in as you are going along.

5 Once it's all rolled up, secure it firmly with a bit of sticky tape.

6 To make the flower petals, choose another colour of crêpe paper. Use the scissors to cut a rectangular piece 20in x 4in (50cm x 10cm).

7 Once you've got the piece cut out, you need to fold it into quarters.

8 Use the scissors to cut around all the edges of the square you have folded.

9 Keeping all the layers together, round off the edges of the square with your scissors to make a rough circular shape. You can cut a perfect circle shape if you'd rather – it all depends how rustic you'd like your finished flowers to look.

10 Using the scissors again, cut into the circle to make the petals. Once again, this can be as neat or as rustic as you wish. It can be good to be a little bit haphazard with your cutting to make the flowers look more natural.

Tip! Try curling the edges of your petals using the edge of the blade on your scissors to make them look a bit more natural.

11 Take the skewer and press through the centre of all the layers. This is making a neat hole for the pollen to be pushed through.

12 Grab the pollen part of the flower and feed the wire through the hole you've just made. Wiggle the pollen part through the flower until just the strands are showing. Pop that to one side and cut a 12in (30cm) length of flower-arranging tape.

13 Give the tape a little stretch to activate it. Starting from the base of the flower begin to wrap the tape around the stem.

14 Continue to wrap the tape further down the stem until it is covering around 2in (5cm).

15 Repeat all of the steps above but using different colours each time to make more flowers for your beautiful arrangement.

Gold piñata

This quick and easy diamond-shaped piñata will bring a bit of razzle-dazzle to any celebration. Made out of a cardboard box, it's the ultimate make for a last-minute surprise celebration. The piñata is fun for everybody – not just for kids.

1 Using a pen, draw out a large triangle 8in (20cm) wide by 9½in (24cm) high onto a piece of scrap paper. Use this template to draw around to create three triangles on the cardboard box.

2 Use the scissors to cut out each triangle.

3 Use strips of masking tape to attach all the triangles together.

WHAT YOU NEED

- [ ] Pen
- [ ] Scrap paper for template
- [ ] Sturdy cardboard box material
- [ ] Ruler
- [ ] Scissors
- [ ] Masking tape
- [ ] Gold thread
- [ ] Gold foil paper
- [ ] Latex-based glue

Tip! To play the traditional game of piñata, fill it with treats before closing the lid and hanging it up, then let everyone bash it to release the treats. But if you prefer to keep your decoration intact, simply hang it up and distribute the treats later!

4 Fold the triangles into a diamond shape and secure with a bit of tape on the inside. Turn it so the point is at the top and place over another piece of cardboard that is big enough to cover the square end. Use your pen to draw around the square and cut out.

5 Use the scissors to push a hole in the centre top of the square piece of cardboard. It doesn't have to be too neat as it will be covered eventually. Use tape to secure the square lid to the side of one of the triangles.

6 Cut a length of thread and tape firmly onto the inside of the square piece of cardboard.

7 Feed the thread out through the hole you made so it is ready for hanging. Use tape to hold the end square to the sides lightly.

8 Take the gold foil and grab your scissors ready to begin cutting out the strands. Cut a long, fairly narrow strip of foil.

9 Cut horizontally along the length of the foil to make individual strips; you can make these as thin or as wide as you like. Make more if you need to.

10 Blob a bit of glue on the top of the strip on the reverse. Stick all around the point of the diamond shape.

11 As you begin to move further up the diamond shape you can start to glue straight along one edge and glue more than one strand at a time.

12 Continue to work up the shape in even lines until all the sides are covered.

13 Once you reach the top, continue to stick the gold strands in a square motion around the end.

14 Continue until the hole of the top is covered, leaving a tiny space for the thread to come out from.

15 Your party piñata is now ready to hang.

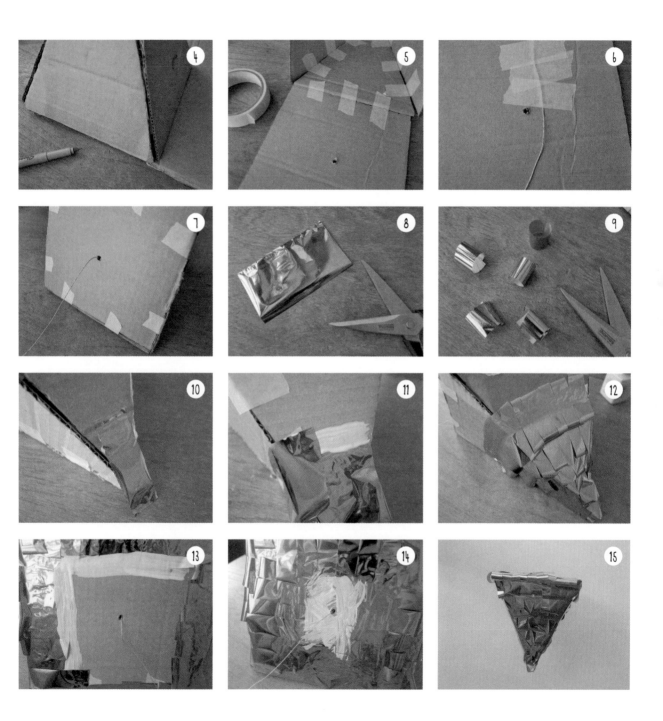

CRÊPE-PAPER FLOWERS, PAGE 58

GOLD PIÑATA, PAGE 62

* < * > *

perpetual creative

* < * > *

Russian doll

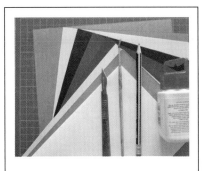

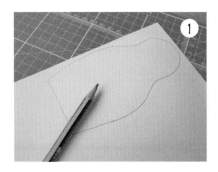

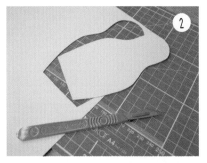

WHAT YOU NEED

- [ ] Scrap paper for stencils
- [ ] Pencil
- [ ] 160gsm A4/60lb US Letter size card stock in beige, yellow, red, blue, green, mauve, black and grey
- [ ] Cutting mat
- [ ] Scalpel
- [ ] Latex-based glue
- [ ] Paintbrush

Inspired by the Russian folk era, this layered paper matryoshka doll makes a welcome addition to any bookcase, or would look lovely hanging up or framed on the wall. A modern twist on a traditional design, this paper cut would complement any space.

1 Trace the main shape of the doll (template A, page 129) onto scrap paper. Lay your stencil over the top of your piece of beige card and trace over it again.

2 Cut out the body shape, making sure you are working on your cutting mat. Use the scalpel slowly and steadily to create an even line. Put to one side for later.

3 Using the yellow sheet of card, transfer the cape and bow (template B) and cut them out. Put these with your first cutouts and save them for later.

4 Now do exactly the same again, but this time with the base (template C) on the red card. Once cut out, put the base with the rest. This piece will form the bottom of the doll.

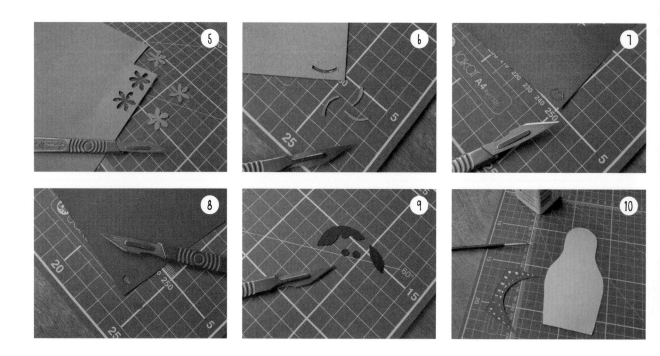

5   Next cut out the small flowers. Using template D, draw three flowers onto the blue card and cut them out. These can be quite fiddly to cut out neatly so they may be a bit rough around the edges. Once cut out, go back round them to neaten them off.

6   Using the green piece of card, trace and cut out the flower stems (template E). You will need three of these.

7   Now go back to the red piece of card and trace out the lips (template F) with a pencil. Cut it out carefully and place it with the others.

8   Using template G and the mauve card, trace out the rosy cheeks and place them with the others.

9   Take the black sheet of card and using template H draw out the hair and eyes, then cut them out with the scalpel. The eyes can be tricky to get the same so it might take a few goes to get them right.

10 Now all your pieces are cut out, you can start to glue them together. We have used the cutting mat, but if you prefer, you can protect your surface with newspaper or scrap paper. Begin with the beige card

cutout and the red base. Using the paintbrush, dab small blobs of glue along the back of the red card. Stick to the bottom of the beige cutout so the two horizontal lines match up.

11 Before you can stick on the hair, you need to line up the cape stencil to mark its position. Use a pencil to draw a faint line around the top of the face circle to make sure you are sticking the hair in the right place. Remove the yellow card to reveal a faint semicircle.

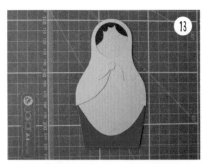
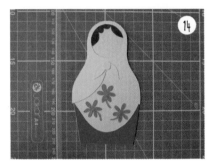

12 Use the paintbrush to dab small blobs of glue onto the back of the pieces of hair. Stick them along the line you have drawn.

13 Next, take the main yellow cape piece and turn it over. Using the paintbrush, dab glue to cover the whole piece. Turn it back over and stick it on the top of the body and hair sections. Push down hard to secure and then stick the bow details on after.

14 Now stick on the flower details. Grab the three flowers and their stems and start by gluing the first stem to the centre of the bottom beige section.

Once the stem is secure, glue a blue flower over the top to create an effective flower design. Stick down the other two flowers to create a pattern. Don't worry if yours is different from this one – you can position the flowers however you please!

15 Now finish the doll by placing and sticking the eyes, lips and rosy cheeks. Dab a bit of glue onto the back of each and position them on the face.

16 You are now ready to stick the whole design onto the grey card, which you can cut to size. Turn over the doll and use the paintbrush to dab glue on the back. Place the doll in the centre of the grey card, push firmly and leave to dry before framing or hanging.

Tip! Once you've made one, make another a bit smaller, then another, and another…

3D lion

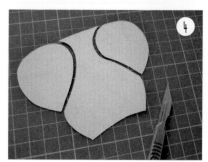

WHAT YOU NEED

- [ ] Scrap paper for stencil
- [ ] 180gsm A4/65lb US Letter size card stock, hammered card in mustard brown, pale brown, pale cream, yellow and black
- [ ] Scalpel
- [ ] Cutting mat
- [ ] Pencil
- [ ] Sticky pads

This lion is given depth by creating a layered cutout. The use of sticky pads between the layers gives the lion a 3D effect. We've also used a slightly hammered card to add texture to the lion's features. This handsome fella would look great in a kids' bedroom or given pride of place in a hallway.

1 Trace template A (see page 130) onto scrap paper. Lay it over the top of the mustard-brown card and trace over it again to create the lion's mane.

2 With the cutting mat underneath your piece of card, use the scalpel to cut out the shape you've just drawn.

3 Transfer template B onto the pale brown card using your pencil to create the lion's hairy face. Use the scalpel to cut out this shape. Take extra care in the curves to create a smooth line.

4 Using the pale cream card, trace and cut around the eyes and cheeks (template C).

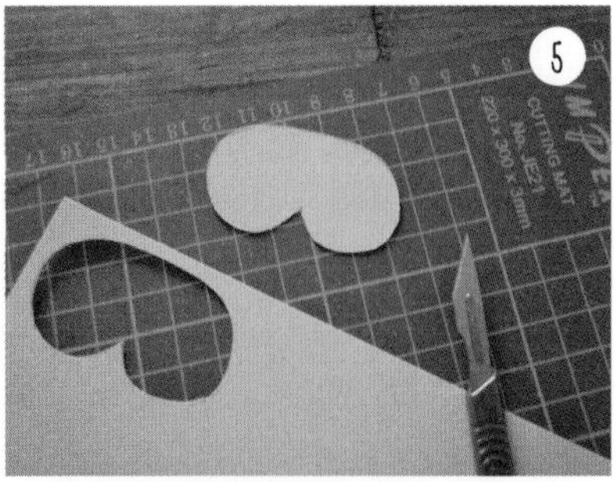
5

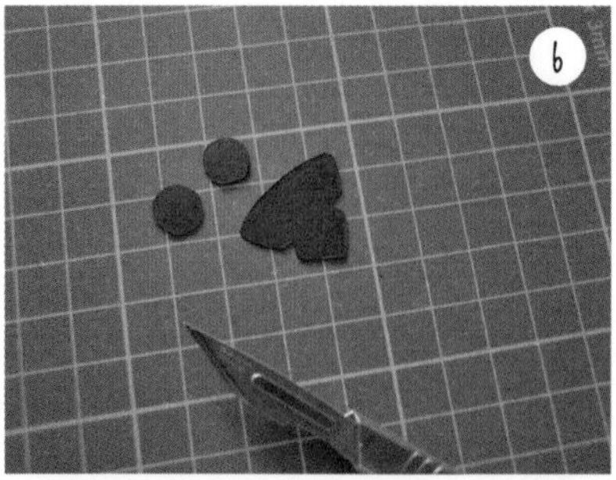
6

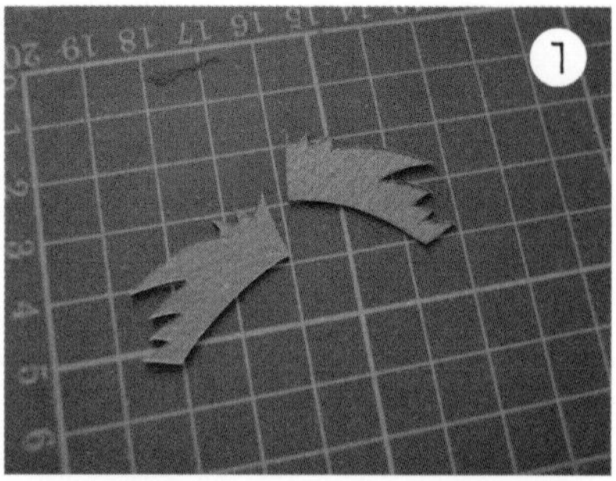
7

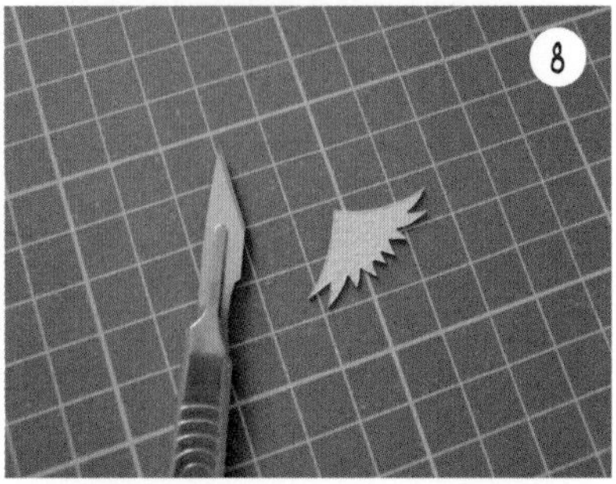
8

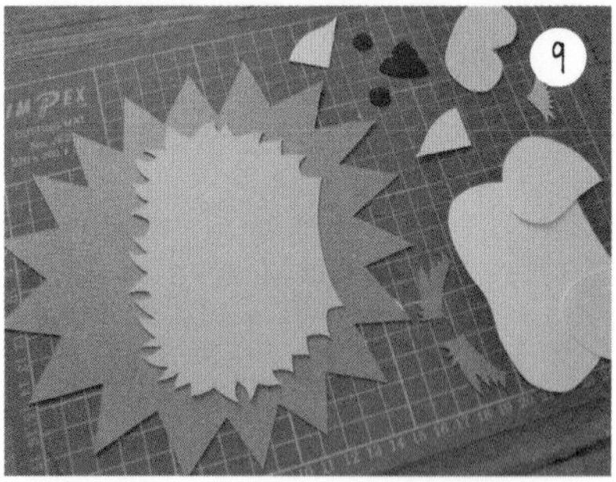
9

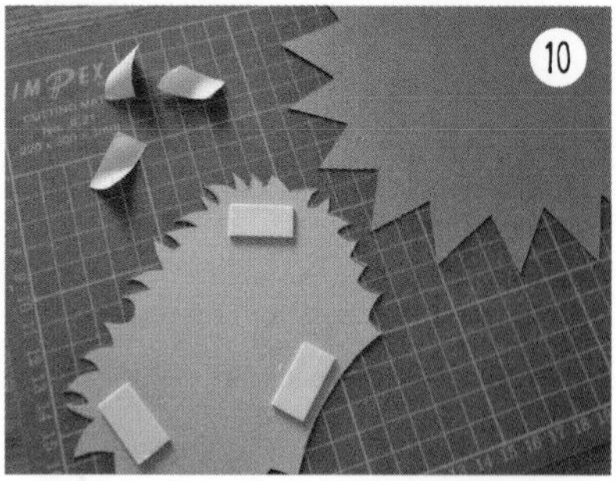
10

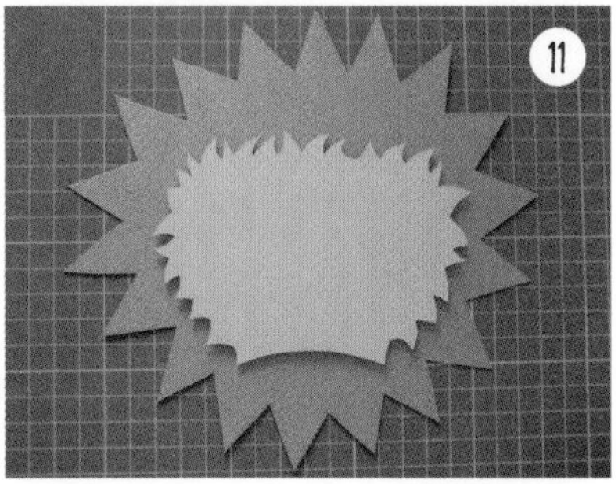
11

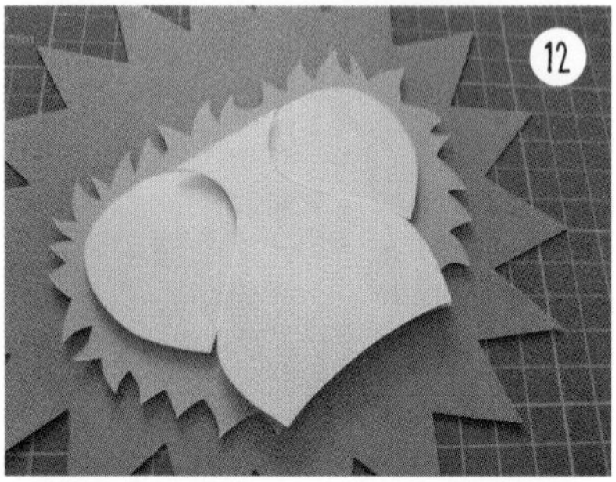
12

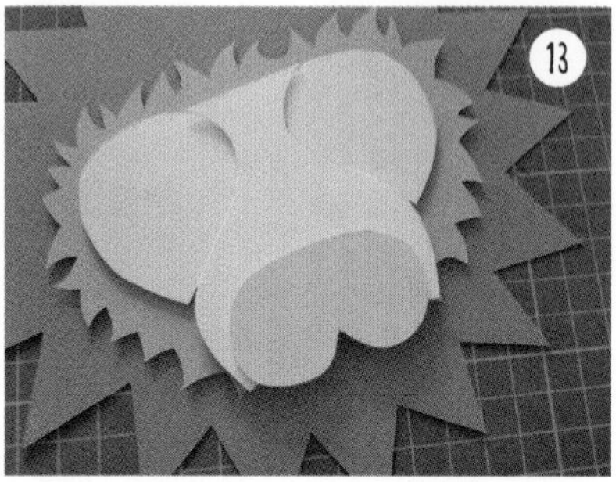
13

14

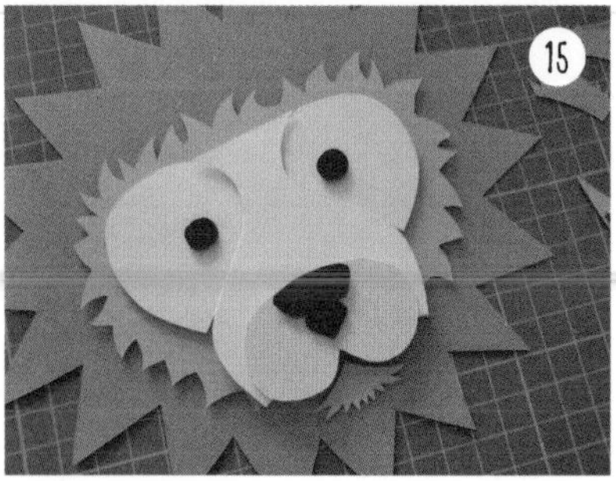
15

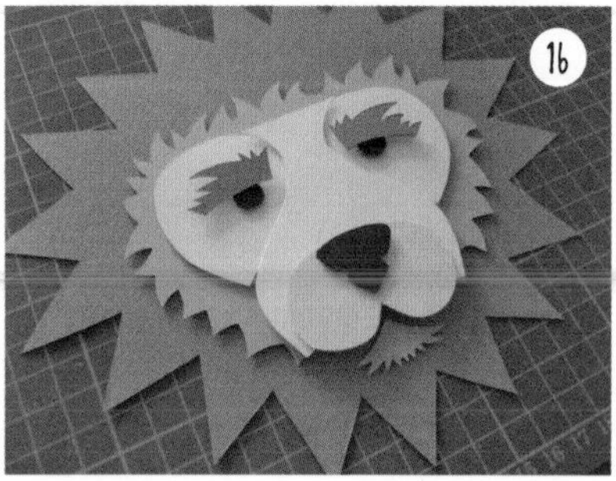
16

Tip! There are quite a lot of pieces to this paper cut, so make sure you keep them all together in a safe place ready for assembling.

5 On the yellow card, cut the lion's muzzle (template D). Put it to one side with the rest.

6 Take the black piece of card now and cut the nose and the eyes (template E). Once again, cut them out as close to the edge as you can.

7 Go back to the mustard-brown card and cut out his tufty brows (template F).

8 Lastly, you just need to cut out his chin tuft (template G), using the piece of pale brown card.

9 Now you've done all the cutting, you are ready to assemble the lion. Start by gathering all the cutouts onto your workspace so everything is close to hand.

10 Start with the face and the mane. Stick down three sticky pads onto the back of the face. Then peel back the top layer on each of the pads so they are ready for sticking.

11 Turn the face back over and place the face on the lower part of the mane. Push down lightly on the sticky pads to secure.

12 Pick up the eyes and cheeks. Start by sticking the eyes down onto the face, using a pad each. You now need to build up a higher layer for the cheeks by placing two pads on top of each other. Peel off the layers and stick in position. This layer should be parallel to the layer underneath.

13 Now you can stick the yellow muzzle, into position. You need to use only one sticky pad for this.

14 As the next pieces to be stuck down are much smaller, take a couple of sticky pads and use the scalpel to cut the pads into small pieces. Start by sticking down the chin tuft underneath the yellow muzzle area.

15 Next you can stick down the black nose detail. Position it so it runs alongside the top of the yellow muzzle area. For the two black eyes, you may need to cut one of the recently cut pads in half again. Use two small pads to stick down the eye detail.

16 To stop the lion from looking quite so startled, you now need to stick down his tufty brows. Once again, you may find it helps to cut the pads even smaller as you need to position the eyebrows onto the eyes.

Cheese-plant phone case

Here at Super+Super HQ, we have lots of plants around the studio. Plants are healthy for the office as they release oxygen into the environment – and this cheese-plant design was very much inspired by this. This upcycled phone case would make a great gift for gardening lovers or just those who love all things tropical.

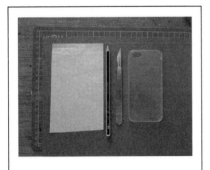

WHAT YOU NEED

- ☐ Scrap or tracing paper for stencil
- ☐ 160gsm A4/60lb US Letter size card stock in forest green
- ☐ Pencil
- ☐ Scalpel
- ☐ Cutting mat
- ☐ Clear, plastic mobile phone case

1 Trace the template (see page 131) onto scrap or tracing paper. Lay your stencil over the top of your piece of green card and trace over it again. You can go over it in pen to make the lines clearer.

2 Lay the scrap paper onto the corner of the piece of green card and press firmly over the stencil with your pencil to indent the card with the design. Once you remove the paper, you should be able to make out the design on the card clearly.

3 Begin cutting out the design, making sure you are working on the cutting mat. You could aim to start in the top right-hand corner, slowly removing any sections in between the leaves as you go.

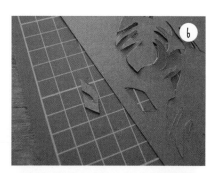

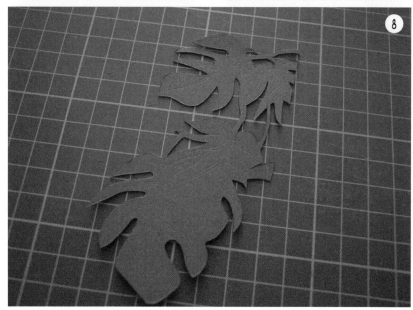

4 Continue to work your way across the outline of the design. Remember to move the paper (rather than your arm) in the direction you are cutting. This will give you more control and help you cut smooth lines.

5 Continue until you've cut the outline of the whole design. Remember to also cut the outlines on the detail on the left-hand side too.

6 Focusing on the left-hand side details again, you can now cut vertically straight down to cut out the leaves as whole pieces. Put these three pieces to one side for later.

7 You now need to cut another vertical line along the edge of the right-hand side of the design.

8 Remove the cutout piece from the rest of the card and place on your cutting mat.

11 Because the phone has a clear case you don't want to use any glue to attach the paper cutting, but once the phone is secure, it's not going to move anywhere. Place the design into your case and remember to add in the extra three leaves on the left that you saved earlier.

12 Once you are happy with the layout and the camera isn't obstructed, click your phone into the case and turn it over to show your design.

9 It's now time to start cutting out the details on the leaves. Refer back to the stencil if your earlier markings are unclear, and start at the top left-hand corner. Continue to make your way down the design, cutting out the leaf details. This can be fiddly as the design becomes increasingly fragile – so take extra care here.

10 Finally, you can cut out the leaf details as well as the leaf edges on the bottom part of the design. When your piece is finished, you can admire your handiwork and grab your phone case ready to pop it in place.

Tip! These phone cases make excellent gifts for your pals. Why not make two and give one to a friend for their birthday?

3D ocean jar

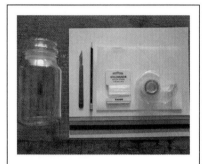

WHAT YOU NEED

- ☐ Scrap paper for templates
- ☐ 200gsm A4/80lb US Letter size card stock in bright blue, white, pale blue, grey, black and orange
- ☐ Pencil
- ☐ Scalpel
- ☐ Cutting mat
- ☐ Sticky tape
- ☐ Nylon string
- ☐ Glass jar, approximately 6in x 4in (15cm x 10cm), with lid

This 3D paper-cut project showcases a fun way to make art and decorate a leftover jar. Bright colours and an ocean scene of ships make it the perfect decoration for your bathroom. Ahoy there!

1 Trace the templates (see page 132) onto scrap paper. Lay your first seascape (stencil A) over the top of your piece of bright blue card and trace over it again.

2 Use the scalpel and cutting mat to cut out the shape from the card. Take extra care to make the curves neat, then put to one side.

3 Now transfer stencil B to the white card to create the second seascape. Use the scalpel to cut out this shape and put it to one side.

Tip! Some of the cuts in this project are quite fiddly, so take extra time and care when cutting out the stencils.

4 For the last part of the seascape, mark out stencil C with your pencil on the pale blue card. Using the scalpel, cut out this shape. Put to one side and get ready to move on to the smaller details.

5 Trace two of the clouds (stencil D) onto the grey card with your pencil.

6 Cut them out with the scalpel, along with the third cloud cut out from the white card.

7 Trace the three birds (stencil E), onto the black card and begin to cut out. These are very small and very fiddly, so take your time. Once you have cut out all three birds, neaten up the edges before putting them to one side with the rest of your cutouts.

8 It's now time to cut out the ships. Take your orange card and transfer onto it your ship stencil (stencil F). Try to get the stencil in the corner of your sheet so you don't waste the card.

9 Begin to cut out the first ship with the scalpel, taking extra care to keep the piece whole.

10 Repeat steps 8–9 so you end up with two orange-card ships. Gather all your cutouts onto the cutting mat, ready for assembling.

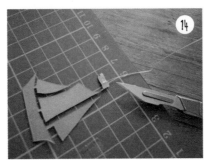

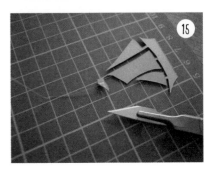

11 Take the bright blue piece of card and stick a piece of tape at one end. Roll up to the width of the inside of your jar and secure with another piece of tape before placing inside the jar.

12 Take the white piece of card and roll it up slightly smaller so it fits inside the blue piece you just put into the jar. Secure with a strip of tape. Pop the white piece of card into the jar inside the blue piece to begin to form the ocean.

13 Repeat the same process with the pale blue card, this time making the roll even tighter so it fits inside the white card. Pop the pale blue card into the jar and place it inside the white piece. These pieces will move around and that's what we want them to do. Moving the jar will move the ocean and these pieces of cards will represent the moving waves.

14 It's now time to start attaching the nylon thread to the hanging parts of the design. Start by cutting a piece of tape around ¾in (2cm) long. Use the scalpel to cut off small strips. Take your first ship and cut off a piece of nylon string about 3½in (9cm) in length. Place the end of the string on ship's pennant, and stick down with the precut tape.

15 Use your knife to cut off any excess tape so there isn't any hanging off the edges. Push down a couple more times to secure the string to the ship. Repeat with the second ship too.

16 Remove the lid from the jar and turn it over. Begin by sticking the ships onto the back of the lid with a piece of tape and continue with the rest. It is, of course, totally up to you exactly where you stick each item and at what height.

17 Now it's time to attach the nylon string to your clouds. Take the clouds and cut three pieces of nylon string 2in (5cm) long. Using the precut pieces of tape, attach them to the back of the clouds. Do the same for the birds, but this time you need 2³⁄₄in (7cm) of nylon string.

18 Collect all the leftover pieces on your cutting mat ready to stick to the jar lid. Using tape, stick the nylon string to the lids the same way you stuck the boats. Once again, the layout is completely up to you.

19 Turn the lid over carefully and ease the hanging cutouts into the jar. Close the lid shut.

20 Your 3D jar is now finished. Give it a little wiggle to see all the pieces move.

Bird wall-hanging

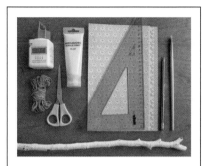

WHAT YOU NEED

- [ ] Tree branch, approximately 16in (40cm)
- [ ] Paintbrush
- [ ] Yellow acrylic paint
- [ ] Set square
- [ ] Patterned A4/US Letter size paper
- [ ] Pencil
- [ ] Scissors
- [ ] Latex-based glue
- [ ] String

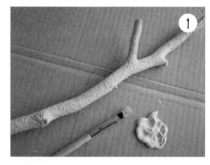

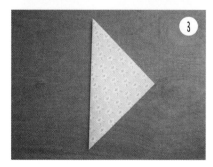

This wall-hanging uses origami to create a lovely piece of wall art. These little birds perched upon their branch would make a great gift for a bird lover.

1 Start by painting the tree branch with yellow acrylic paint. Continue painting the branch until it is completely covered and leave to dry for two hours. Give it another coat if necessary and leave until it is completely dry.

2 Using the set square, measure a 15cm (6in) square onto the back of one piece of patterned paper and mark out with your pencil. Use the scissors to cut out the square you've just drawn.

3 We're now going to start folding a bird. Begin by folding the piece of paper in half, patterned side out.

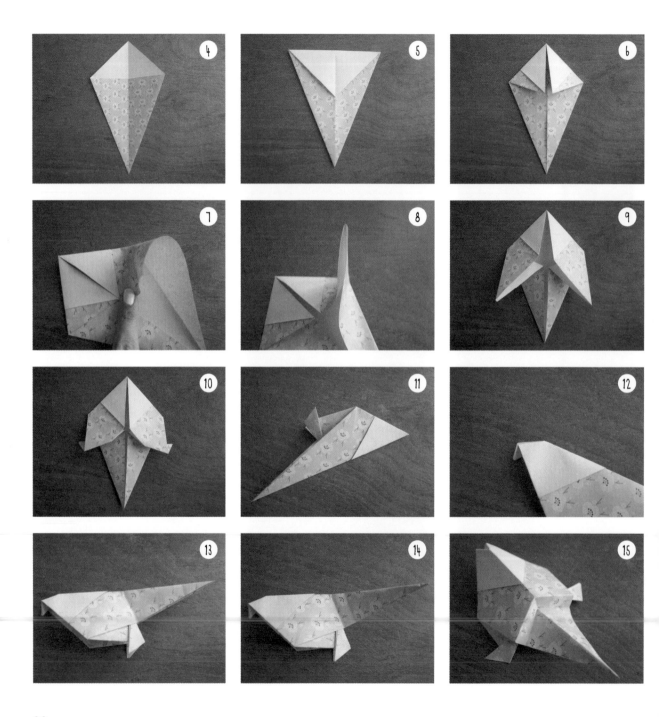

4 Open up the paper and fold the right-hand side into the middle crease. Then fold the left-hand side into the middle to meet the crease as well.

5 Turn over the paper and fold the top half down.

6 Turn the paper back over and fold down the right top corner to the middle. Fold in the opposite corner to meet in the middle.

7 Open out the right-hand side and fold over the top piece of the paper to form a white square.

8 Pinch the rest of the right-hand side of the paper in order to form a standing structure.

9 Fold this structure down flat to form this shape. Repeat on the other side.

10 We're now going to construct the bird's feet. To do this, simply pinch and fold the right-hand point round to the back. Repeat on the other side. Your paper will now slightly resemble a frog, but that's a good sign!

11 Turn the paper over and fold the design in half. You'll start to notice it's now representing a bird shape.

Tip! Once you've got the hang of this origami bird, see what other origami animals you can make and create your own unique wall-hanging.

12 Turn the bird to face you and pinch in the top to create the beak. Lay it back on the table and flatten down to complete the distinct beak shape.

13 Fold the tail over towards you and over the bird to create a straight fold down the legs of the bird. If you open out the fold, you will see a defined line.

14 Fold the tail back over again, but this time ³⁄₈in (1cm) short of where you just folded it. If you open out the fold, you will see two folded lines on the tail.

15 Open out the bird design slightly and pinch the tail to push back into the two folds you've just made.

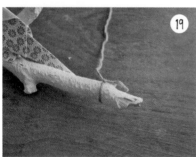

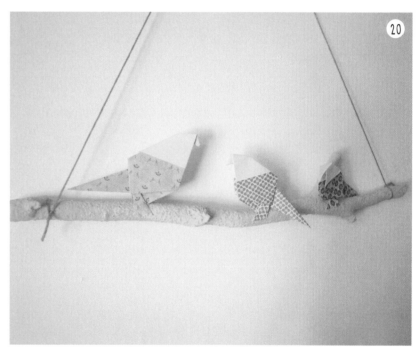

16 Turn the bird onto its side and flatten. The tail can now be pushed in and out slightly according to how tall you'd like it to stand.

17 Repeat all these steps with different patterned paper and different sizes. Try making them with 4¾in (12cm) and 4in (10cm) squares.

18 To attach the birds to their branch, blob a tiny bit of glue onto the branch to begin with. Open the bird up slightly and place the legs either side of the branch, press onto the glue and hold until secure. Stick down the other birds in the same way.

19 Tie the string to either end of the branch and fix with a bit of glue if necessary.

20 Your wall-hanging is now ready to hang up.

Tip! Make sure the wall-hanging is completely dry before you hang it up.

3D LION, PAGE 74

CHEESE-PLANT PHONE CASE, PAGE 78

committed crafter

Paper-cut bunting

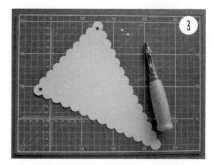

Make your own personalized bunting for a birthday, wedding or just for fun! This project is quite a lot of work, but you can always keep coming back to it until it's finished. Hang it high and hang it proud. After all, it took you a lot of time and cups of tea to make.

1 Trace the bunting flag shape template (see page 133) onto scrap paper with a pencil. Lay the stencil over the top of your piece of card and trace over it again. Each piece of card can hold two flags.

2 Place the card onto your cutting mat and use your scalpel to begin cutting out the first bunting shape. The trick here is to take it slow and steady, as curves can be tricky. Move the paper, rather than your arm, in the direction you wish to go. This will help you to stay more controlled.

3 Continue to work your way around until you have cut the whole piece out. Take the Japanese screw punch and punch two holes in the top corners of the bunting. This is for the string to be threaded through. If you don't have a screw punch, just one end of a normal hole punch will do fine.

WHAT YOU NEED

- [ ] Scrap paper for stencil
- [ ] 180gsm A4/65lb US Letter size card stock in white
- [ ] Pencil
- [ ] Cutting mat
- [ ] Scalpel
- [ ] Japanese screw punch (or hole puncher)
- [ ] String

Tip! Two flags fit on each piece of card so make sure you get enough card for the number of letters you need.

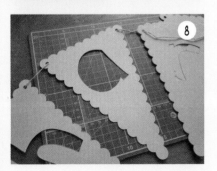

Tip! If you don't have time to do the bubble edges, cut some simple triangle shapes instead.

4 Trace your first letter onto scrap paper with a pencil (see pages 133–135) and transfer it to the middle of your first flag.

5 Use the scalpel and cut out the letter. If you cut it out in one piece you can keep the inside letter for a future project.

6 Repeat steps 1–5 until you have cut out all your flags and letters. If you have an 'and' in your design why not use the '+' stencil provided to save a bit of time?

7 Once all your flags are finished, arrange them in order with the first letter at the top. Then take some string and feed through the first hole from front to back.

8 Bring the string through from the back into the second hole in the first flag and repeat this process until all your flags have been strung together. Your bunting is now ready to hang.

Bicycle paper cut

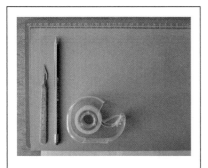

This single cutout is the most detailed and time-consuming of all the projects in this book. Inspired by the work of fine artist Rob Ryan, also known for his paper-cut work, its intricacy is not one for the faint-hearted. However, once complete it's something to behold. Try showcasing it in a picture frame under clear glass or perspex.

1 Trace the template (see page 136) onto tracing paper using a pencil, and go over the bicycle with a pen so the design is clear. Pick up your scalpel and prepare yourself to begin cutting!

2 Starting at the bottom left-hand corner, cut around the edge of the leaves. Continue to cut around the edge of the top of the bike and around the section in between the gears and the grass. Remove this section carefully.

3 Now cut a line along the bottom of the whole design. This is a freehand line that was not on the original template, so pencil in where you want to cut. To be in keeping with the rest of the design there's no need for a ruler.

WHAT YOU NEED

- ☐ Tracing paper for stencil
- ☐ 160gsm A4/60lb US Letter size card stock in grey
- ☐ Pencil
- ☐ Pen
- ☐ Sticky tape
- ☐ Scalpel
- ☐ Cutting mat
- ☐ Picture frame

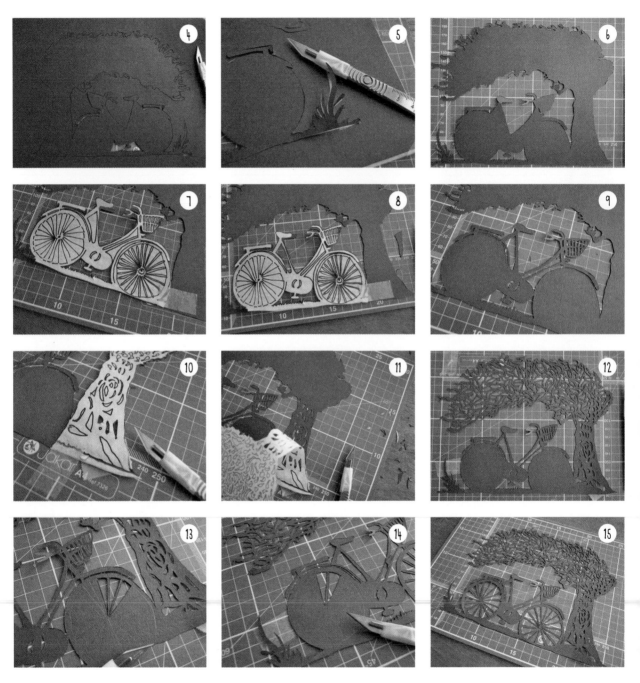

Tip! Don't forget, you can fix any mistakes with a tiny piece of sticky tape. See page 27.

4 Starting from the tree, continue to cut around the edge of the whole design. Turn over the card once you have completed this to see if there is anywhere you've missed.

5 While it's turned over, use the scalpel to neaten up any edges or missed spots to remove the design from the rest of the card.

6 Once removed, turn the design over ready to begin with the details. Remove the tracing paper and keep it to one side, as you'll need it later.

7 Tear the bike design part of the tracing paper off and stick it back onto the paper with a small piece of tape. Stick the tape to a jumper or a fabric surface a few times before you stick it to the card to make sure it's less adhesive – this is so you don't rip the card when it's removed.

8 Now cut out a few of the bike details. Start with the space in between the rear wheel and saddle.

9 Cut out the space between the front two bars, the holes in the gears and the basket details, and remove the tracing paper to reveal.

10 Take the rest of the leftover tracing paper and secure it to the design with more slightly fluffed tape. You can also stick the card to the mat with one piece of tape if you find the design slipping around too much. Begin to cut out the tree.

11 Continue to cut out these details going up the tree. You can peel back the tracing paper at any point to see your progress.

12 Continue to work across the tree, making sure to take regular breaks to rest your wrist. Once you've cut the rest of the tree out, take a step back and admire all your precision cutting. Pop the kettle on for a tea break if you haven't done so already.

13 It's now time to cut out the bike wheels, but first you need to draw on the wheels. Grab your pencil and draw on the bike spokes. You can make them as simple or as detailed as you like. Using the scalpel, start to cut out your first wheel.

14 Move over to the next wheel and repeat the same process.

15 Your single cutout is now finished! Pop it in a frame to protect it and hang it with pride.

Picture-frame window art

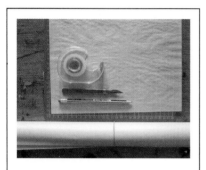

This fun picture-frame window art is a welcome addition to any window. The decorative sticker is the ideal way to add a bit of joy to a back-door window or a child's bedroom. The frosted effect means it still lets in light – and it's removable too.

WHAT YOU NEED

- [ ] Sticky tape
- [ ] Tracing paper (four pieces)
- [ ] Pencil
- [ ] Pen
- [ ] A3/US Tabloid size frosted window vinyl
- [ ] Cutting mat
- [ ] Scalpel

1   Use sticky tape to attach all four pieces of tracing paper together. Trace the templates (see pages 137–138) onto tracing paper using a pencil, and go over with a pen on each tracing so the frame is clear.

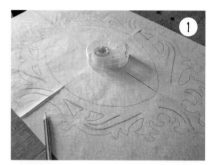

2   Place the tracing paper on the back of your window vinyl and secure with some sticky tape, ready to cut.

3   Use your scalpel and begin to cut along the outline of the design, making sure you are pressing hard enough to go through both the tracing paper and the vinyl.

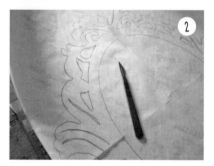

Tip! Try going to your local hardware store and looking in their bargain bin. You can get offcuts of window vinyl at super-cheap prices!

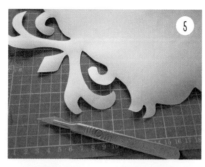

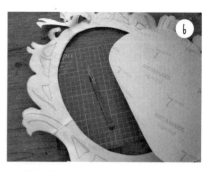

4 Continue cutting all the way around the outside edge of the whole frame.

5 Once you've cut the whole piece out, remove it from the rest of the paper and neaten up any edges if they need it.

6 Use your scalpel to cut out the centre of the frame and remove – save this piece to make something else at a later date.

7 Starting from the left-hand side, begin to cut out the frame details.

8 Once you reach the bottom, take extra care with the long, thin curved lines as they can be quite fiddly.

9　Repeat on the right-hand side and discard all the sections you have cut away.

10　Your window vinyl is now finished! All you need to do is peel off the backing and stick to a window of your choice.

Tip! If the tracing paper has fallen away, you need to stick the inner piece back onto the frame design to continue cutting out the details. Just use a few little bits of tape to secure it on.

Constellations plate

WHAT YOU NEED

- [ ] Tracing paper
- [ ] Pencil
- [ ] 180gsm A4/65lb US Letter size card stock in black
- [ ] Cutting mat
- [ ] Scalpel
- [ ] 180gsm/65lb card in gunmetal grey
- [ ] A plain china plate for decoration
- [ ] Paintbrush
- [ ] Spray mount glue
- [ ] PVA glue
- [ ] Plate or palette

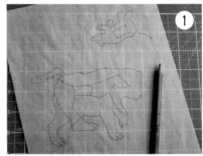

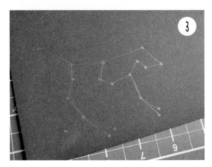

Inspired by the stars and space, this project creates a decorative plate that features two constellations: the Ursa Major and the Ursa Minor, also referred to as the Great Bear and the Little Bear. These guys would look great on a side table with your keys in or as a decorative plate on the wall.

1   Trace the template of each bear (see page 139) onto tracing paper using a pencil.

2   Take the piece of black card and lay it on the cutting mat. Place the tracing paper on the card so that the constellation part of the stencil on the larger bear is close to the edge. Again using a pencil, push hard over the lines of the constellation to create an indent in the card underneath.

3   If the markings aren't clear enough for you to work on the black paper, draw them in with a pencil.

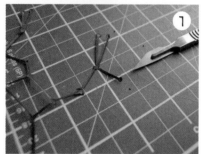
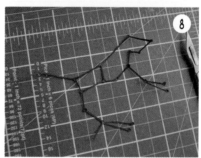

4 Beginning at the bottom left-hand part of the design, use your scalpel to start to cut out the straight lines of the constellation. Continue to work up the leg – the lines you are making should be about 1/8in (2mm) wide so they will not break.

5 Carry on until all the straight lines in the design have been cut out.

6 You can now cut out the circle parts of the constellations. The middle section of the design can also be removed with the scalpel.

7 Once you've finished, the whole piece can be removed from the rest of the card. Take some time to even out the circular shapes to make them as neat as possible.

8 Once the constellation is finished, pop it to one side for later.

9 It's time to cut out the constellation for the smaller bear. Place the tracing paper design on the black card again and press hard over the design with a pencil.

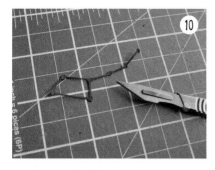

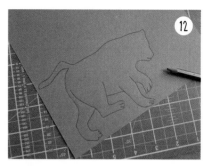

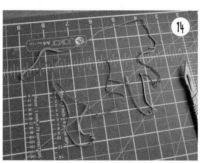
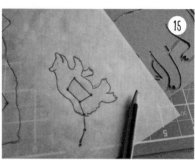

10 Remove the tracing paper and draw over the design with a pencil if you need to. Cut out the piece in the same way as before, doing the straight lines first. Neaten up the circles, once they are removed from the rest of the card. Put it to one side for later.

11 Place the stencil over the grey card and draw over the bear shape with your pencil.

12 Remove the tracing paper and go over the outline with a pencil on the grey card if you need to.

13 Starting at the tail, use your scalpel to begin to cut out the larger bear. Once again the lines need to be about ⅛in (2mm). Keep going round the whole design until the bear is cut out.

14 Remove from the rest of the card and neaten up any edges.

15 Repeat the steps with the small bear design and the grey card.

Tip! Your plate is a decorative item, so don't immerse it in water or put it in the dishwasher.

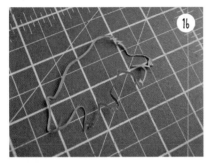

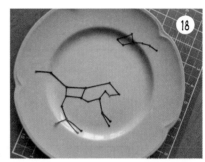

16 Remove from the card and neaten up any stray edges.

17 On a protective surface, turn over the small constellation so it is the wrong way around and from a distance of around 12in (30cm), spray a coating of spray mount.

18 Turn over and stick onto the plate. As this part is on the edge make sure you press down firmly to ensure it is stuck down smoothly. Repeat the steps for the larger bear constellation.

19 You can now follow the same steps to stick down the bear designs over the top of the constellations Remember to turn them over and spray glue on the underneath so they are the right way round when you stick them down.

20 Squeeze out some PVA onto an old plate or palette and have your paintbrush at the ready. Spread a thin layer of PVA glue across the whole plate. Don't worry if it starts to dry patchily; eventually it will dry completely clear.

Scandinavian lampshade

WHAT YOU NEED

- [ ] 180gsm A4/65lb US Letter size card stock in pale yellow
- [ ] Set square (or ruler)
- [ ] Cutting mat
- [ ] Scalpel
- [ ] 180gsm A4/65lb US Letter size card stock in lilac
- [ ] Sticky tape

Inspired by Scandinavian design, this line-shape lampshade will add a touch of style to any hanging light. Simple to hang and made from two pieces of card, it's thrifty style at its best.

1 Place the pale yellow card horizontally on your cutting mat. Starting ³⁄₈in (1cm) in from the edge, to cut a line cut that is 2¹⁄₂in (6cm) long using a scalpel.

2 Move the set square down ¹⁄₈in (2mm) and do another 2¹⁄₂in (6cm) long cut. Do this until you have 20 identical cuts, each ¹⁄₈in (2mm) apart.

3 Beginning with the top two lines, do two small vertical cuts in between each at either end. Remove the shape you've just cut.

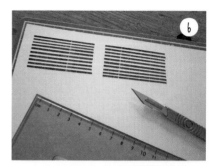

4 Repeat this step going down until you've cut and removed 10 line shapes.

5 Align the top line with your set square or ruler and measure ³⁄₈in (1cm) before doing another 2³⁄₈in (6cm) cut.

6 Repeat steps 2–4 until you have another section with 10 line shapes removed.

Tip! For safety, use only an LED light in your lampshade as it creates much less heat than regular bulbs.

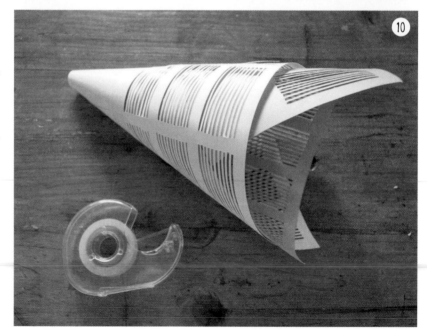

7   Once again, from the top line move across ³⁄₈in (1cm) and cut out another 10 shapes. Continue working along until you have four blocks cut out and the whole length of the card is covered. Measure down ³⁄₈in (1cm) and cut another four blocks horizontally along the page. Measure down another ³⁄₈in (1cm) and cut out another four blocks.

8   Take the lilac card and lay it vertically on the mat. Down the right-hand side you will be doing six more blocks of cuts. For each block do 20 line cuts each ⁵⁄₆₄in (2mm) apart as before. Cut them into 10 removable lines as you have done previously.

9   It's now time to assemble your lampshade. Wrap the lilac card around the top of the light cord. Fix with one small piece of tape.

10 Wrap the yellow card over the lilac card so the bottom edges are asymmetrical. Fix with another small piece of tape.

BICYCLE PAPER CUT, PAGE 100

SCANDINAVIAN LAMPSHADE, PAGE 114

····· **bits and bobs** ·····

Templates

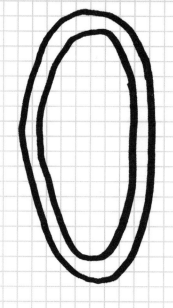

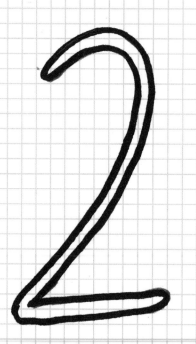

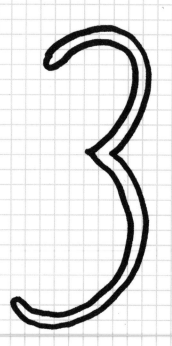

Birthday-cake toppers, page 32.

Copy these at 100%

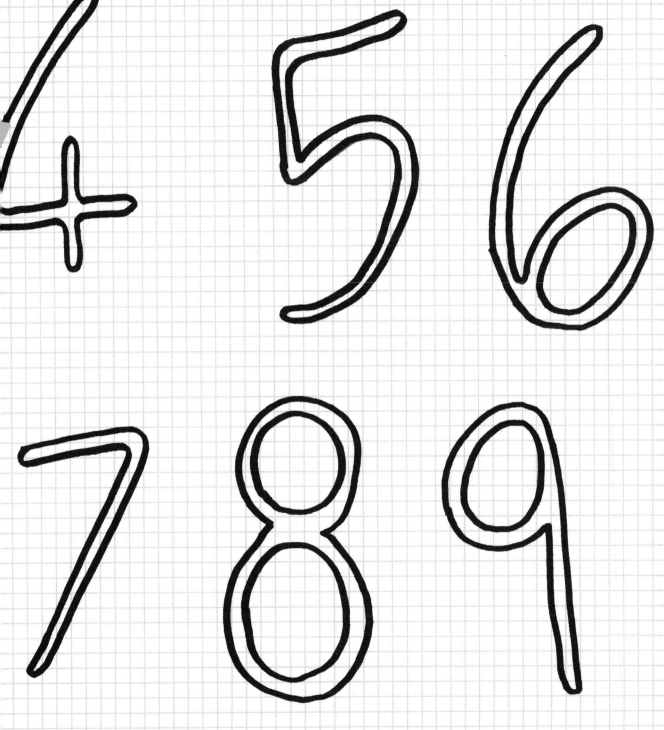

Party props, page 34.

Copy these at 200%

Valentine's cards, page 38.

Copy this at 100%

Blackboard stickers, page 40.

Copy this at 200%

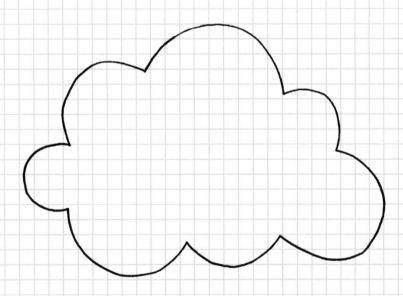

Cloud baby mobile, page 50.

Copy this at 100%

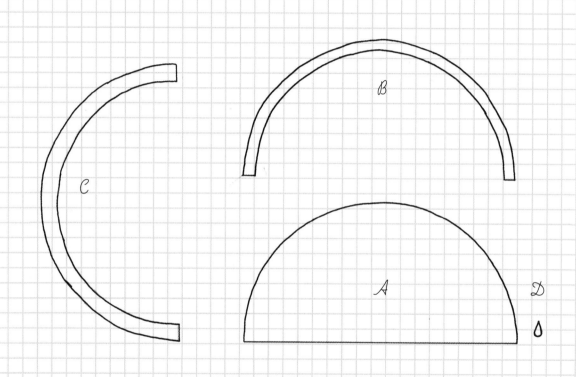

C

B

A

D

Watermelon stationery set, page 55.

Copy these at 200%

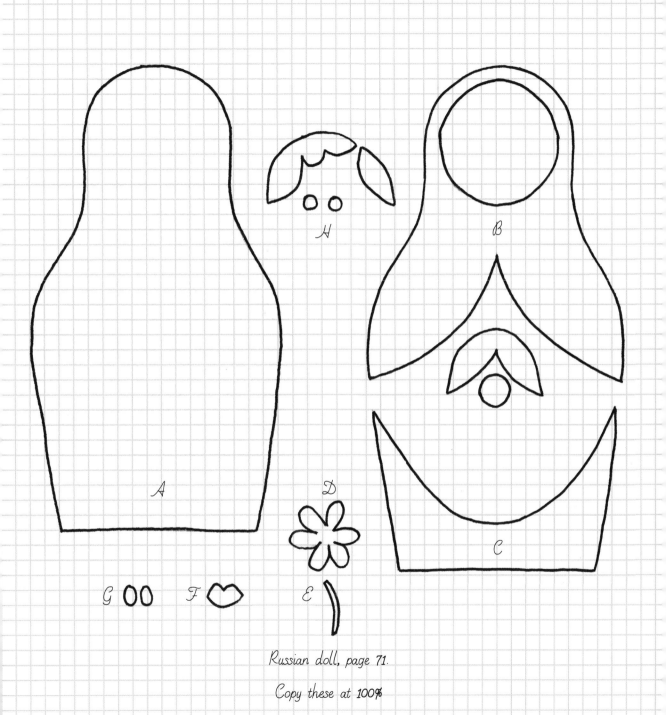

A

H

B

D

E

G OO

F

C

Russian doll, page 71.

Copy these at 100%

A

F

E

G

D

B

C

3D lion, page 74.

Copy these at 200%

Cheese-plant phone case, page 79.

Copy this at 100%

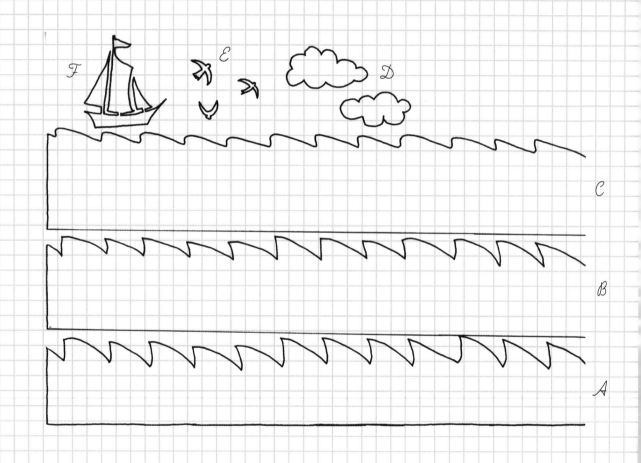

F E D C B A

3D ocean jar, page 82.

Copy these at 200%

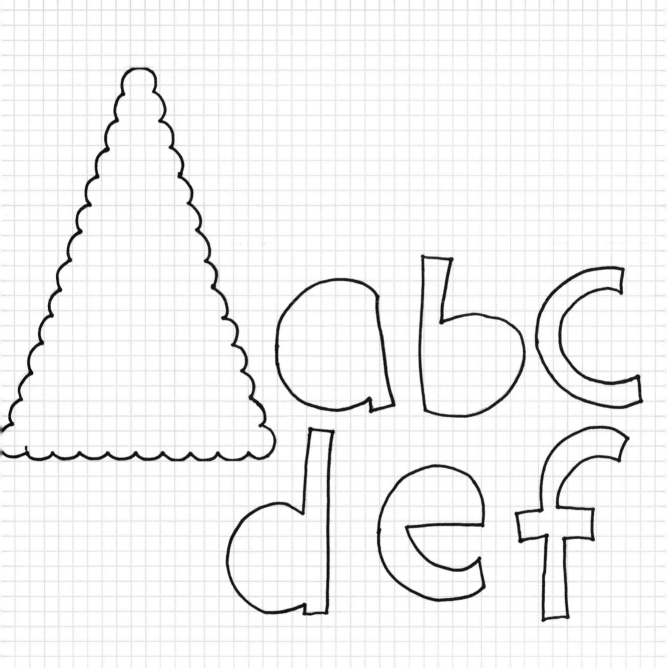

Paper-cut bunting, page 98.

Copy these at 200%

ghij
klm
nop
qrs

Paper-cut bunting,
page 98.
Copy these at
200%

Paper-cut bunting, page 98.

Copy these at 200%

Bicycle paper cut, page 101.

Copy this at 150%

Picture-frame window art, page 104.

Copy this at 200%

Picture-frame window art, page 104.

Copy this at 200%

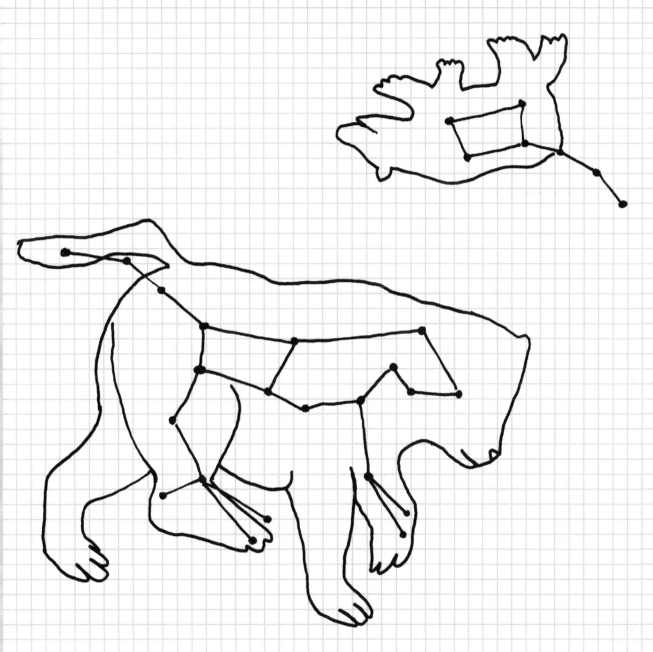

Constellations plate, page 109.

Copy this at 100%

Resources

suppliers

Amazon
www.amazon.co.uk

Eco-craft
https://secure.eco-craft.co.uk

Hobbycraft
www.hobbycraft.co.uk

Paperchase
www.paperchase.co.uk

Ryman Stationery
www.ryman.co.uk

Staples
www.staples.co.uk

WH Smith
www.whsmith.co.uk

inspiration

Craftgawker
www.craftgawker.com

Jessica Das
www.jessicadas.com

Kate Spade Advertising
www.katespade.com

Lisa Rodden
www.lisarodden.com

Lou Taylor
www.lou-taylor.co.uk

Mr Yen
www.mr-yen.com

Pinterest
www.pinterest.com

Rob Ryan
www.robryanstudio.com

Yuko Yamamoto
www.yukoyamamoto.jp

events

AOI Illustration awards
www.theaoi.com/events

The London Illustration Fair
www.thelondonillustrationfair.co.uk

Pick me up
www.pickmeuplondon.com

Acknowledgements

We are so happy to see the Super+Super series provide such inspiration to all you crafty people out there. It really is a joy for us to see everyone making these ace projects. We'd like to take this opportunity to thank each and every one of you who has bought this book. You are personally responsible for making our dreams a reality.

We'd like to thank all our friends and family for supporting us through this venture and for listening to us talk about these books for hours on end. You really are super.

We'd also like to thank our cats for providing us with hours of comfort and attention.

Index

To order a book, or to request a catalogue, contact:

GMC Publications Ltd

Castle Place, 166 High Street, Lewes, East Sussex

BN7 1XU, United Kingdom

Tel: +44 (0)1273 488005

www.gmcbooks.com